THE
FOLKLORE
OF BIRDS

THE
FOLKLORE
OF BIRDS

The forgotten tales behind nature's
most enigmatic creatures

ALISON DAVIES

Illustrated by
Sarah Wildling

Leaping Hare Press

Contents

Foreword

I have adored birds for all of my life. As a child I was fascinated by their plumages and wondered why you never saw naked birds. I marvelled at their different shapes, sizes and hues. How could a basic, although unique, biological design featuring a beak, wings and feathers have such a wealth of different varieties? And of course, there was the one thing that completed the circle of love that I had for these beings; their vaunted ability to fly. But loving all things birds has always been about more than just their physical presence in our world.

For me, one of the biggest attractions that birds held were the wonderful stories attached to them that traversed back to ancient times. Stories that illustrated the wonder and, often, respect that we had for these amazing creatures. My introduction as a child was to read and collect poems penned by the likes of John Keats, Thomas Hardy and other lesser-known poets. In reading these works I came to realise that some featured fables surrounding the species or bird family that they wrote about. This discovery marked the beginning of my deep interest in the legendary status of some of our most enigmatic bird species. Learning about mythical birds like the phoenix was one thing, but discovering the stories and mythology handed down by our forefathers and foremothers was spellbinding.

Enter Alison Davies and her wonderful book. This is a woman who is truly in love with birds and the natural world. Her choices of species that she has featured are very interesting. They are about birds that many of us would have at least heard about. They are birds that despite their familiarity have held a fascination for humankind since the dawn of time. Some of the stories told around the birds have inadvertently led to them being protected, to a degree. Others, namely the owls and crows, have almost universally had bad press from day one. Recounting the fables surrounding these families of birds may help shine a very bright light on the futility and stupidity of the more negative stories. I hope that those stories will inspire and galvanise readers to look at these, and indeed all, birds with different eyes. But it is the younger minds that need to be the most inspired. Minds that are full of wonder and open to considering notions that as adults we are often closed to.

As such, this book is a very important one. I hope that Alison's words supported by Sarah Wildling's beautiful illustrations will help to spread the conservation message that we all so need to heed. The blend of factual information that melds into their evolutionary path that, in turn, leads us to the fable and myth is a wonderful story. I love this approach. It adds colour and depth to the stories of these magnificent birds that you would not readily get elsewhere. Now learn about and enjoy the wondrous world of birds!

David Lindo aka **The Urban Birder**

Introduction

My fascination with birds began in early childhood, ignited by my dad's made-up bedtime stories, based around the character Rob the Robin, a tiny red-breasted hero who had a penchant for saving the day and lived in the Wild Woods with a whole host of other creatures. While I enjoyed the stories for what they were, my interest in our feathered friends steadily grew and I started taking notice of our regular garden visitors.

Fast forward to my twenties, and my love of all things avian had expanded to include birds of prey, in particular owls of every shape, size and species. This was no doubt enhanced by the presence of a little owl at my bedroom window; a face-to-face encounter that seemed to go on for an eternity, and will stay with me for just as long. Add to this the rich seam of folklore from around the world, the superstitions and myths, both good and bad, and I, like the prey they so cleverly lift from the ground, was hooked. I could empathize with the ancients who must have looked at these winged wonders and believed they were witnessing something mystical. After all, these mighty birds with their sharp steely eyes could fly, bringing them closer to the heavens than any human at that time, and that was only the beginning of their gifts.

The more I learnt about all types of birds, the deeper I wanted to go, uncovering the narratives that informed the folklore and understanding what those early civilizations saw. And so, years later, the idea for this book, which combines both fact and myth, was born. Like the birds that feature in these pages, I feel I have travelled the globe, albeit from the comfort of my desk, to discover what makes them tick and why we feel the way we do about them.

Berated birds like the magpie, so often maligned for its opportunistic behaviour, have charmed me with the care they demonstrate to each other and in parenthood, not to mention their uncanny street-sense and the startling realization that silvery objects repel, not attract them in droves. The vulture, with its scary demeanour, is so far removed from the horror of this world, and clearly the top of the tree when it comes to saving the environment. The pigeon too is a champion, saving lives not just in times of war, but today through its keen senses and internal compass. And these are just a few of the species that have made me think again.

Some birds are obviously more appealing, being aerially gifted or able to belt out a symphony with gusto from dawn to dusk. Then there are those with a striking plumage, the glorious peacocks of the world with their many-eyed tails, or the delicate, brightly patterned goldfinches, a garden treat that can easily be encouraged with the offering of some Niger seeds. For me personally, it's the birds that are overlooked or dismissed that are the most magical. The pheasant, for example, is a most misunderstood game bird on UK shores, but go further afield and you will find an altogether different perspective. In Japan these birds are revered, after the fiery shape of one graced the skies thousands of years ago. There are revelations within the pages of this book, along with tales, superstitions and myths, that will make you see that nature is extraordinary and should never be taken for granted.

Birds represent freedom and a lightness of being that defies the laws of gravity. With this in mind, I hope you enjoy the selection of birds on offer here, and that the words and beautiful illustrations inspire you to experience and nurture these winged miracles.

BIRDS
OF
PREY

Whether among the clouds, out at sea or hovering by the wayside, these majestic birds wear their predatory presence with ease. There is no need for loud introductions or a fanfare. Such enigmatic raptors prefer to remain incognito, coasting the updrifts looking for the optimum chance to pounce. But while they are gifted on the wing and able to navigate the skies with grace, they also have a tale to tell. From the king of the birds – the striking golden eagle, almost angelic in form and structure – to the twisting, turning kestrel – a bird that inspires romance thanks to its wind-hovering dance – you will find a selection of birds of prey to fall in love with in this chapter, and you will discover why these warriors of the wing have captured the hearts and minds of humans for centuries.

GOLDEN EAGLE

FAMILY: *Accipitridae*

DISTRIBUTION: Eurasia, North America and North Africa

HABITAT: Mountainous areas, desert tundras, grassland, farmland, coniferous forests and alongside rivers

Majestic and mighty, the eagle swoops upon a current of air, its outstretched wings creating a gentle V-shape. It has a wingspan of up to 2.3 m (7.5 ft) and fierce, gleaming eyes, large in comparison to other birds. The golden eagle's eyes are at least four to eight times more powerful than our own, and they also have the ability to see in full colour. Then there is the bill; sharp and hooked, and stronger than it looks, this bird uses it to clasp its prey and sometimes deliver a terminal blow to the nape of the neck.

These birds may be killing machines, but there is something enigmatic about their presence, an underlying energy that has enthralled humankind for centuries. Indeed, the eagle is an ancient species, with the oldest fossil findings discovered in a dried-up lake in Australia. The remains are thought to be around 25 million years old, and depict a type of eagle which has been called *Archaehierax sylvestris*, meaning 'hawk of the forest'. While the bird is smaller than the golden eagle, it has prominent features that prove it was a distant ancestor. Fossils from other Aquila-type birds have been discovered in parts of Europe, while golden eagles have been identified at Rancho La Brea, in California, in 20,000–40,000 year old Pleistocene asphalt seeps.

The fifth-century Roman poet and historian Pliny claimed that a golden eagle was responsible for the death of the

Greek playwright Aeschylus. His demise was apparently foretold, and it was predicted that he would meet his end when something fell upon him. To avoid such a catastrophe, Aeschylus spent a lot of time outdoors, and it was on one such sojourn that a golden eagle swooped low and dropped a tortoise on his head. Eagles eat a range of prey, including smaller birds, fish, reptiles and mammals such as hares, prairie dogs, squirrels and marmots. Luckily this incident, which is well documented in history, did not deter the Romans from taking the bird as their mascot, particularly in battle. It became an insignia, often raised on standards by the legions, to represent courage and as an emblem of the city of Rome.

The Egyptians were equally smitten with the eagle, and it appears as a hieroglyph that represents the letter A on the Rosetta stone. The steppe eagle was the bird of choice of the pharaonic civilization, most likely because it was a common visitor to Egyptian skies, migrating there every year. This enormous bird was thought to represent Upper Egypt, and was loosely linked to the goddess Nekhbet. Often depicted on temple walls and in tombs, the winged goddess was associated with protection.

Hunting with eagles was a popular pastime for early tribes. In remote parts of Mongolia it was a traditional practice, used for centuries to supplement food during the harsh winter months. Eagle hunters trained the birds, usually golden eagles, to seize prey and bring it back to order; in return, the bird would receive a part of the prize for its trouble. This practice is still popular today, and carried out in Kazakhstan, Kyrgyzstan and Mongolia.

In Native American tradition the eagle holds great significance. Its ability to soar among the clouds and see further than any other bird makes it a king among birds. The bald and the golden species in particular are revered, and thought to represent courage, honour, power and freedom. Feathers from these birds hold a special medicine which makes them powerful, and are considered a sacred gift.

In Norse mythology the eagle was synonymous with the god Odin. Its plaintiff cry was thought to herald the birth of a great hero, while to the Celts these birds were omens and messengers of the gods. Should a solitary eagle be seen resting upon a rock, then an enemy was close at hand; however, if you were lucky enough to spot two eagles together, then peace was within your grasp.

The golden eagle is the national bird of Mexico, Albania, Germany, Austria and Kazakhstan, making it the most common national animal in the world.

♦

They are skilled hunters, and the force of their talons has been likened to the impact of a bullet hitting the skin. When they dive in for the kill they can reach speeds of up to 241 km/h (150 mph).

♦

They are choosy when it comes to home-making. Golden eagle pairings will construct several nests within their territory, but they tend to use only one. The nests are called 'eyries', and they are built high up on trees, rocks and cliffs.

♦

These birds like to dance. Golden eagles perform a courtship ritual known as 'sky dancing', which involves a series of jumps, dives and dips to impress their mate. Couples also play with sticks and dead prey, throwing them into the air and catching them as they fall.

VULTURE

FAMILY: *Accipitridae*

DISTRIBUTION: Vultures are found on every continent except Antarctica and Australia

HABITAT: Deserts, savannahs, grasslands and open mountainous regions

Skating on an updraft of air, the vultures circle. Theirs is a slow and steady pattern painted upon the horizon that makes the most of thermal air currents, allowing them to travel greater distances without having to dip into precious energy supplies.

Vultures have been misjudged for centuries. They might not be blessed in the looks department – most species have a bald head and neck, with a large looming wingspan and a sharp curved beak – but these hefty carrion eaters are essential to the eco system. Vultures feed on rotting carcasses, recycling the nutrients from the meat and preventing the spread of infectious diseases.

Divided into two distinct groups, there are Old World vultures which hail from Africa, Asia and Europe and are closely linked to raptors and other birds of prey, and there are New World vultures found in North and South America. These birds are related to the stork, and have a keen sense of smell which they use to hunt for food. Turkey vultures, in particular, have the largest olfactory system of any bird, and can sniff out a carcass from around a mile away. Old World vultures are blessed with excellent sight. They use their exceptional vision to track predators, such as wolves and foxes, in search of their next meal.

Old World vultures are blessed with strong, sturdy feet and talons, which give them a secure grip and the ability to run over rugged terrain. New World vultures are not so lucky. While their feet can brace a dead body, they are much weaker and tend to flap awkwardly, hopping short distances, giving them a somewhat comical appearance. These birds also lack a voice box, which means they can only make hissing and grunting noises. Old World vultures do have a voice box, and are unusually vocal when feeding. They have been known to croak, rasp and screech, while white-backed vultures have a habit of squealing like a pig when they are enjoying a meal. Both types of bird have a robust immune system which allows them to tuck into spoiled meat; this coupled with strong stomach acid means the carcass is swiftly digested.

Vultures have a long history with humans. One of the world's oldest musical instruments, discovered in a cave in Germany, dates back to around 33,000 B.C. and is an ancient flute fashioned from a vulture bone. Many civilizations revered the vulture, believing it was a sacred symbol linked to purification. The Romans even kept various body parts and bones for medicinal purposes and as talismans for good health and protection. They associated the bird with war and military precision, a belief which was based upon the vulture's presence at the battlefield. As such, this carcass-feeder became associated with the god of war Mars, and was often seen as a positive omen by soldiers going into battle. Indeed, the founder of Rome, Romulus, cited the bird's presence on the Palatine Hill, as a sign that this was the spot where the founding city should be built.

In Egypt, the bird was associated with royalty and considered sacred to the ancient Pharaohs. The Egyptians believed that all vultures were female, and so the birds were synonymous with motherhood and a symbol of the mother goddess Isis. They were also deified in the form of the vulture-headed goddess Nekhbet, who governed and protected Upper Egypt. It was thought that she could transform into a griffin vulture, and in this form she guided the souls of the dead. The cult of Nekhbet was a popular one, and priestesses would adorn themselves with white vulture feathers as a way of honouring both the bird and the goddess.

Feared and revered throughout history, the vulture's popularity may dip and soar, but its fate will always be intertwined with humankind.

Vultures' gastric acid is stronger than battery acid, with a pH of a little over 0. The acid dissolves any bones that they consume, and also kills anthrax and botulism.

♦

Their baldness makes it easy for the sun's rays to disinfect their skin.

♦

A group of vultures circling overhead is known as a 'kettle'. If the vultures are perched together in a tree, they are often called a 'committee', 'venue' or 'volt', and if they are feeding together, they are known as a 'wake'.

♦

Vultures vomit when they are under attack. These unique birds have the ability to vomit mid-flight, which reduces their body weight, helps them flee and acts as a deterrent.

KESTREL

FAMILY: *Falconidae*

DISTRIBUTION: Widespread throughout Europe, Asia and Africa, and North America

HABITAT: Farmland, heath, moor, grasslands, urban and suburban habitats

Skating on a breeze, hovering mid-flight, the kestrel has only one thing in mind: its next meal. Keeping its head perfectly still during this aerial spectacle, this sharp-eyed hunter is able to peruse the landscape for a tasty meal while delicately treading air. With the ability to see prey from around 50 m (164 ft) away, this bird's vision is eight times more powerful than our own. Once the prey has been pinpointed, the kestrel will swiftly pounce, dropping soundlessly to snap up its quarry. These clever birds like to cache, so they will often catch several voles at a time and store some for their last meal of the day.

Small but perfectly formed, with pointed wings and a long tail which fans out when the bird is in hover mode, the kestrel is a falcon belonging to the genus Falco. While its origins are sketchy, it is thought the bird originated in Africa and then spread across the Old World. The American kestrel is the exception; this colourful bird has a reddish tinge to its back and tail feathers, and grey-blue wings and head, while the common kestrel, also known as the Eurasian, is slightly larger and less colourful. Even so, the male of the species still sports a grey-blue head, but its plumage is light brown and mottled with darker spots. The female is dowdier in appearance, being mostly brown.

Ardent when it comes to love, the kestrel usually mates for life, although some males do take more than one female during a breeding season. They usually begin their courtship during the winter, as this allows them to develop stronger bonds ready for the coming spring. This, along with the name 'Windhover', a moniker given because of this falcon's ability to ride the wind and hover in one place while hunting, only serve to add to its romantic reputation. Indeed, the Victorian poet Gerard Manley Hopkins was so inspired by the flight of the kestrel that he wrote the sonnet 'The Windhover', paying homage to the bird's aerial dexterity.

Despite the ingenuity it displays, medieval falconers were not so impressed, believing it to be inferior to other larger birds of prey. As such, it was the choice of lowly knaves with lesser falconry experience. The kestrel was seen in a different light by the ancient Egyptians, who prized the bird for its ability to traverse the skies, and associated it with their sun god Ra. The recent discovery of a mummified kestrel in a tomb serves as evidence that falconry was a popular pastime of the higher echelons of society. The ancient Greeks believed the bird to be associated with Zeus, who would often change into a bird of prey. Kestrels were seen as friendly, helpful spirits, because they assisted in keeping pests at bay, like locusts.

To the Hungarians, the kestrel was synonymous with divination, and associated with the mythical Turul, a falcon-like bird that appeared in a dream to the wife of an ancient ruler. The mystical creature blessed her with a vision of the future, which showed she would be the matriarch of a long line of powerful rulers. Asian folklore also recognizes the bird's sharp intellect and ability to see from a great height, believing it be a visionary. It is thought that seeing a kestrel is a sign of good things to come. That said, this falcon does not fare as well in Japanese mythology, with one folktale citing a kestrel-like bird with wings and tail feathers made of swords as the villain who chased a local warrior from his bed. Perhaps the bird's ability to appear out of nowhere, riding the wind and then diving deep for its prey made it seem somehow menacing to early civilizations, who believed all birds were messengers from the heavens. Either way, the kestrel remains an enigmatic bird, and a favourite of many birdwatchers who enjoy watching it surf the sky.

Kestrels are lazy when it comes to nest-building, preferring disused crows' nests, empty tree cavities, cliff ledges and even buildings.

♦

The best place to spot them is on or near a motorway, where they can be seen looking for prey along the verges. They also favour telephone posts, where they can perch and get a clear view of their surroundings.

♦

In the Seychelles, kestrels are synonymous with death. It is believed that should you hear the cry of one at night in your garden or upon your roof, then a member of the family will soon pass away.

♦

Males are called 'tercels', which comes from the Latin term *tertius*, meaning 'third'. This originated from the old belief that only one in three kestrel eggs would turn out to be male.

OSPREY

FAMILY: *Pandionidae*
DISTRIBUTION: Found on all continents except Antarctica
HABITAT: Near oceans, rivers, lakes, reservoirs, coasts, lagoons,
estuaries, reefs, swamps and marshes

A solitary glider takes to the skies. Its powerful wings are angled, creating an M-shape from beneath. This bird is in no rush as it soars above the ether. With its pale mottled belly and dark upper wing feathers, it is easy to spot. Couple this with the stark colour combination of a white head and the distinctive brown eye-stripe and you will know that this vision is an osprey.

This stunning bird of prey may be large, but it has a slender body and wings and is often mistaken for a gull in flight. These birds prefer the shallower depths when it comes to catching prey. Gifted with an acute focus, the osprey has two fovea in each eye. These deep impressions in the retina are filled with colour cones which keep their vision sharp and give them a wide field of view. Humans only have one fovea in each eye. Once a suitable fish has been isolated, the bird will angle its dive for maximum success, plunging into the water with its legs and talons extended. Ospreys, unlike many other birds, do not cache their food, and while they prefer a live fishy snack, their diet is diverse and can include snakes, birds, frogs, reptiles and small mammals.

Ospreys are resourceful and can live in range of environments from the icy cold temperatures of the Arctic Circle to the intense heat near the equator. This adaptability goes some way to explain their worldwide distribution and longevity through the ages. Fossils were discovered that show these birds existed around 10–15 million years ago, and they are mentioned in the Bible. Even so, the birds were rare on UK shores up to the early 20th century, having been persecuted for many years. Their adept fishing skills put them at risk, with fishermen feeling the impact on the numbers of salmon and trout. As a solution, the birds were regularly shot and their eggs kept or destroyed. Along with natural changes to the habitat and the spread of disease, it meant that by 1847 ospreys were extinct in England and Wales. Scotland swiftly followed suit. While the birds still made the occasional isolated appearance, breeding pairs were a thing of the past until a couple of Scandinavian osprey changed the fate of the species in 1954. This industrious pair raised their chicks close to Loch Garten in Scotland and the first brood resulted in a gradual increase in breeding birds.

Steeped in myth and legend, it is no surprise these powerful raptors have a range of names and tales associated with them. Their genus Pandion is a direct link to King Pandion of Athens. Grandfather of Theseus, the king appears in a legend where his two daughters and evil son-in-law Tereus are all turned into birds by the gods. Tereus becomes a hawk, constantly chasing the two women through the skies.

The ancient Chinese philosopher Confucius claimed that 'the cry of the osprey is joyful without being wanton and sad without being distressing' – a piece of wisdom influenced by the bird's behaviour and a lesson in being both prudent and thoughtful in the way you express yourself. He was not the only Chinese scholar to look to this bird for creative inspiration. The early Chinese folk poem, 'Guan Ju', which appeared in an ancient anthology of work from the seventh century B.C. talks of the cry of the osprey and is one of the most famous poems in Chinese history.

To the Native Americans this bird had a powerful medicine, teaching them lessons in patience and mastery. Most tribes, particularly coastal tribes who had seen the bird's hunting skill and measured flight, believed the osprey was a spiritual guardian, watching over the people. The bird's presence was often seen as warning of danger to come.

Today the osprey is a delight when witnessed traversing the skies or swooping in for a fishy feast. While it may outdo local fishermen with its hunting skill, its presence is a reminder that there is place, space and succour for every creature upon our planet.

Ospreys are usually solitary birds, but a group is known as a 'colony'. Another popular name is a 'duet' of ospreys, a nod to the pairings they make during the breeding season.

♦

They build their nests in trees, on rocky outcrops, cliffs and also manmade structures. Known as 'eyries', they are constructed with twigs and sticks and lined with bark, vines and algae.

♦

Males can get carried away with nest building, sometimes bringing so many sticks back to the nest that he buries the female.

♦

Ospreys do not drink water; their diet of fish gives them all the hydration they need to survive.

BARN OWL

FAMILY: *Tytonidae*
DISTRIBUTION: Found on every continent except Antarctica
HABITAT: Farmland, grassland, woodland and moorland

The soundless flight of the owl is ethereal when witnessed first-hand. This elegant, and often enigmatic, bird has a long and mysterious history. Indeed, the first and earliest owl fossil is an isolated leg bone, thought to be around 60 million years in age. This means the species was in existence at the beginning of the Palaeocene Epoch. Interestingly, those first birds were much larger than the ones we see today. One in particular, a giant type of barn owl, existed during the Pleistocene Epoch which was between 2.6 million to 11,700 years ago. Thought to be around 0.7 m (2.3 ft) in height, with a wingspan of 1.5 m (4.9 ft), this enormous predatory raptor fed upon smaller birds within the same species as well as other raptors and mammals. The Ice Age put an end to this whopping beauty, but it was only the start for the owls, who would evolve into around 250 different species worldwide.

While each is distinctive in nature and form, they all bear some similarities, having long, rounded wings, a shortish tail and sharp, powerful talons. Owl eyes are fixed in position by a bony tube, and so the birds must turn their heads to see their surroundings. They have the mobility to rotate 180 degrees in either direction, allowing them to see directly behind themselves.

Barn owls' heart-shaped faces help to direct high frequency sounds to their ears, allowing them to pinpoint the exact location of their prey. Then they will swoop in silently on soft downy feathers, grab their prey and consume it whole.

Interestingly, barn owls only came to nest in barns around 5,500 years ago. Before this, they were cliff dwellers. When early humans began to construct buildings to keep their crops dry, these resourceful birds saw an opportunity to live in a degree of comfort and safety, swapping their old hang outs for barn rafters.

Known for their infamous screech, and often nicknamed 'screech owls' because of it, the barn owl issues this call most often during mating season. The tone of the screech reveals the sex of the caller, with females being high pitched in sound and shorter lived, to the longer, harsher call of the male. This disturbing cry is not the only way the males charm their mate; they will also present her with 'gifts' in the form of small rodents. Once a pairing has been made, it is usually lifelong and the couples will stay in contact outside the breeding season, although they may inhabit separate roosts.

The barn owl's indominable screech is at the root of many superstitions, particularly in Europe where this haunting scream was seen as a bad weather omen. More ominous still, should it fly past the window of a sick person, it was sign that death was imminent. English literature did not favour this owl much, either, citing it as a bird of darkness, no doubt because of its nocturnal behaviours. The poets Robert Blair and William Wordsworth did their bit to contribute to this, by claiming it was a bird of doom. Despite the barn owl's sinister reputation, many old English folk remedies recommended the use of its eggs. If a child ate them raw, it was said that they would always be protected from drunkenness, while the eggs when cooked to ash were thought to improve eyesight.

In ancient Greece, the owl was synonymous with wisdom and protection, and the little owl, often seen flying around the

Acropolis at that time, was considered to be the bird of the goddess Athena. As such, it was a positive omen, especially when viewed by soldiers going in to battle. The Celts called the owl 'the corpse bird', believing it signified death, while the Vikings held a different view. They saw the owl as a symbol of good fortune, synonymous with knowledge, and the ability to see into other realms.

Around the world, a hooting owl was a sound that would stop many in their tracks, but while our ancestors might have seen this as an omen or a way of keeping evil at bay, today we acknowledge it as a natural wonder and a blessing from this feathered mystery.

Barn owls' ears are lopsided, helping them to distinguish exactly where a noise is coming from.

♦

They tend to eat their prey whole and then regurgitate the fur and bones in perfect little packages called pellets.

♦

While these birds mate for life, there is a tendency for the males to have more than one female partner.

♦

A group of owls is called a 'parliament'. This term was given because they were thought to be wise and intelligent, thanks to their wide-eyed charms.

♦

British barn owls have snowy white chests, while those who hail from Central and Eastern Europe are dark yellow in hue.

CORVIDS

Whether clustered together surveying the landscape from a lofty vantage point in the trees or meeting for a quick and lively exchange which often results in ruffled feathers, the Corvidae family like to be heard. These clever birds are something of a mystery, which is no surprise when you consider their ancient roots. The problem-solvers of the avian kingdom like to make their mark. Glossy black ravens and their smaller crow counterparts feature in myths from around the world. These denizens of shadow made perfect heavenly companions, and like their cousins – the jay and the magpie – they were quick to pick up on any wrongdoing. Should there be a sniff of intrigue, it would pique their interest and have them hopping from foot to foot. Today, they mix it up, sometimes going solo to visit gardens and parks, or travelling further afield in family flocks. These mercurial birds confuse and fascinate in equal measure.

CROW

FAMILY: *Corvidae*

DISTRIBUTION: Found on every continent except South America and Antarctica

HABITAT: Woodland, farmland, grassland, heath, wetland, urban and suburban areas

The glossy black plumage of the crow, along with its stocky build and gleaming dark eyes, give it a mystical bent – as if it is cloaked in shadows. Indeed, this intelligent bird is often hailed as the keeper of secrets, which is quite at odds with its attention-seeking caw.

Raw intelligence shines through its eyes, and it is blessed with creativity and the capacity to problem-solve. Scientists have discovered that crows originated on an archipelago in north Australia, which today would be New Guinea. While most birds born to an island habitat are happy to stay put, often causing a species decline, those first crows were curious, deciding instead to spread their wings and venture over water to wider expanses of land.

A complex bird, the crow can be both solitary and social. It tends to live in family groupings much like humans, and the older offspring help to raise each new brood. It also mingles with larger factions and will roost in flocks. It is a creature of routine, often rising and flying out to forage at the same time of day, then returning to the roost mid-afternoon. Adept at making tools, crows have been known to take a twig, strip it of leaves, then bend the end with their beak and use it as a hook to prise a tasty morsel from a crevice. Researchers from the University of Oxford have also discovered that crows have a sense of numbers and can quickly decipher clues and assemble tools.

Like the raven, the crow has an excellent memory for faces, and will hold a grudge for more than its lifetime, even passing this information on to its young who continue the resentment with renewed vigour. This ability to communicate and learn from each other is unique to crows and ravens. It can even develop positive relationships, learning to trust and reward the hand that feeds. The 2015 story of an eight-year-old girl in Seattle who received the gift of a selection of silver trinkets from the wild crows she was feeding, proves this point.

The crow has always had a mysterious reputation, most likely because of the charcoal darkness of its feathers and its startling caw. Around the world, the crow is associated with death. The Japanese believed the crow carried the souls of the dead to their final resting place, meaning it was not only a guide but also a portend of doom. To the Greeks, most commonly, this bird was linked to the story of the sun god Apollo and his mistress Coronis, who decided to ditch the deity for a mortal man. The crow, who was then white in plumage, brought this fateful news to Apollo. Enraged by the turn of events, the god took his anger out on the bird, singeing its feathers black. Other versions of the same tale make Coronis pay for her betrayal by being transformed into a black crow. From this point on the ancient Greeks believed that a pair of crows signified forbidden love, and the name Corone became the Greek word for crow.

In Celtic mythology, the crow, like the raven, is associated with the goddess of war and death, the Morrigan. She is often accompanied by this bird, or believed to shapeshift into its form, particularly when rifling through the bodies of the dead. In Europe during the Middle Ages, crows were thought to be messengers of the devil, making them the witch's cohort. Their black plumage did not help, and many believed that they were witches in disguise who had taken a bird-like form to escape persecution. In Slavic folklore, the crow is often linked to Baba Yaga, a scary sorceress who lived in a cabin in the woods and ate small children for breakfast. Some argue she was really a wise forest spirit who protected the wild ways and was used by parents to teach their children respect for the natural world.

Crows mourn their dead. They will gather together and hold vigil over the body of another crow, often in silence, as if grieving a loved one's passing.

♦

Crows have clever ways of catching food. Not only will they steal food from other birds, even following them back to the nest, but they will also lure prey using bait. The American crow has a habit of doing this, using pieces of bread to attract fish to the surface of the water.

♦

Crows are organized. They cache their food, often leaving markers on top of hiding spots so they can find it quickly and easily.

♦

They are long-lived. In the wild, crows usually reach the age of twenty years, with some lasting beyond this. In captivity they live even longer, with the oldest known captive crow reaching the grand age of fifty-nine.

RAVEN

FAMILY: *Corvidae*

DISTRIBUTION: Found throughout the northern hemisphere, including
North America, Europe, Asia and North Africa

HABITAT: Woodlands, coniferous forests, rocky coastlines, arid
deserts, mountains, farmland, urban and suburban areas

As old as time itself, the raven in some cultures shaped the world and everything upon it. Even if the folklore is not to be believed, the very presence of this bird is enough to secure its mystical reputation; a fact that is taken quite literally by the British monarchy, who house several of the birds at the Tower of London. According to folklore, should there ever be less than six in residence, then both the tower and the kingdom would fall.

Covered from head to toe with charcoal black feathers, the raven is sturdy in body and shape and much larger than its crow cousin. Bright, beady black eyes and a long, sharp beak signal a bird that can look after itself. Couple this with its ability to thrive in almost any habitat, and you have one of the many reasons for its widespread distribution and success.

Ravens adapt, which is no surprise when you consider the intelligence of this massive passerine. Whether they are in scrubland, wasteland or high upon a mountain, they work with what they have, foraging for scraps, grubs, grain, berries and small mammals and birds. These birds are scavengers at heart and rascals in spirit. Known for their playful temperament, they are often witnessed performing aerial stunts together, sparring and passing twigs, feathers and other simple tools back and forth in flight. Scientists have observed the problem-solving abilities of these clever birds, and have discovered they are gifted mimics, like other corvids. With a vast repartee of over one hundred vocalizations, ravens can copy human speech, sing and will even call to other birds within their grouping when they have found food. No wonder they have lived in abundance alongside us for thousands of years.

To some, ravens are comical, but when challenged they can attack, particularly if they are guarding a nest of young chicks. Gifted with an episodic memory, ravens have the ability to remember faces and also emotions associated with them, which means they can hold a grudge. If a raven has been slighted it will recall the event and feeling for up to a month afterwards. In youth they are sociable birds, preferring the company of other young fledglings before they pair off. Once in these groups, they are called an 'unkindness' or a 'conspiracy', which seems harsh for such a fun-loving bird, but does go some way to serve their dark reputation. Add to this their deep throaty call and a love of carrion, and you can see why the ancients cited them as an ill omen. Many cultures believed the raven was synonymous with psychic power and wisdom, and gave it the moniker, 'The Keeper of Secrets'.

To the Celts the bird was associated with the battlefield, as it was a common sight picking its way through the dead and dying. Because of this, it quickly became linked to the goddess of war and death, the Morrigan. It was thought that she would visit dead warriors in the guise of a raven, to console and soothe them. In Norse mythology, the great god Odin would wander the realms with a raven upon each shoulder. The two birds, whose names were Huginn, meaning 'thought', and Muninn, meaning 'memory', would fly out into the world each day gathering news for their master.

The Inuits believed the raven was a trickster, and were wary of its unpredictable nature. They would never harm the bird, but if they found a dead one, they might use its skin to make clothes for their young, believing that the child would inherit the raven's ability to hunt and find food anywhere. The blackness of this bird's plumage was also a distinctive feature often mentioned in folklore, with many narratives claiming it had been burnt while trying to steal the light of the sun.

In Sweden, it is thought that if a raven croaks at night, it is most likely a murdered soul who has not had a Christian burial.

♦

Ravens love ants, and not just to snack on! They seek out ant hills and will roll in them, causing the ants to swarm over their body. Scientists believe that the ant secretions may soothe the bird's moulting feathers, as well as acting as a fungicide.

♦

White ravens do exist. They are incredibly rare and the result of a genetic disorder known as leucism.

♦

Ravens do not like cheats! These birds often work together to collect food, but if they see another raven taking more than its fair share, they will shun it.

EURASIAN JAY

FAMILY: *Corvidae*

DISTRIBUTION: Found in Europe, West, East and Central Asia, North Africa and the Indian subcontinent

HABITAT: Mixed forest and grassland; jays also favour oak woodland and more urban settings such as gardens and parks

The beautiful jay is a blaze of colour as it scouts the woodland for acorns to stash away. From a distance you might think this bird has mousy brown feathers, but if you look closely, you will see a flash of salmon pink, with criss-crossed azure blue and black wing feathers peeping from beneath the monochrome upper feathers. This sneaky streak of brightness means it is often mistaken for something more exotic, but while the jay may not hail from the Amazon, it is a unique and incredibly intelligent species.

A noisy bird, scientists have discovered that vocal jays feel a range of emotions from love and joy to anger and fear. Unlike other birds, their intelligence is evident in their careful food planning, hunting down acorns and hiding them away for consumption at a later date. Canny jays also have the ability to discern their partner's tastes, and male jays will often return with foodie gifts in the form of the female's favourite berries or seeds, in a bid to keep them sweet.

Jays are excellent mimics and will copy the calls of other birds. This is something they do to throw predators off the scent. American blue jays have perfected this art, and can mimic the call of a much bigger bird such as an eagle or a red-tailed hawk when they feel under threat. They also mimic human sounds, and if they are kept in captivity will often copy their owners as a way of being accepted into the family group. While the Eurasian jay is not a migratory species, they have ventured further afield more recently, thanks to deforestation. The breeding population in Europe alone is estimated at 7,480,000–14,600,000 pairs.

The showy good looks of this avian charmer have always made it stand out from the crowd, and during the nineteenth century nobility would collect the feathers and wear them as vibrant accessories. The Duchess of Edinburgh, Maria Alexandrovna (1853–1920, daughter of Tsar Alexander II and wife of Prince Albert, Queen Victoria's second son), was a huge fan and famously had a muff made entirely of jay feathers. The blue jay was considered lucky by many early civilizations – no doubt the vibrant sky-blue of its plumage was enough to lift the spirits on a dour day. The loud vocalizations of these birds also link them to communication and many mythologies cite jays as messengers between the planet Earth and the spiritual realm.

The sky-bright colour of blue jays also links them to the heavens and spiritual progression, but while they are generally considered a positive omen, African-American folklore sees these eye-catching birds differently. According to one old tale, the blue jay was the first bird to bring dirt to the world when it was covered in water. This in itself was a good thing as it helped to shape the planet, but despite the resourceful nature of this bird it was viewed as a trickster character, with fickle behaviour. Some stories even suggested that every Friday the blue jay would bring twigs to fuel the fires of hell and keep them burning. Native American tribes also viewed the blue jay as a troublesome character. Being noisy and aggressive, they had no time for its negative antics and believed the bird to be an omen of bad things to come.

In truth, most species of jay are fearsome when it comes to protecting their territory – and in particular their own nest – from predators. They will make an enormous amount of noise to distract any potential attackers. It is this protective nature, along with a keenness to learn and adapt, that help these stunning birds survive and thrive in abundance.

In medieval times, a gossip was called a 'jay' after this noisy bird, and if a man abandoned his monastic order and turned to slanderous ways, he too was likened to a jay that had escaped the captivity of a cage.

♦

Blue jays are not blue. They get their hue from a pigment called melanin which is brown, but the way it is distributed through their body means that when the light hits, it looks a vivid blue colour.

♦

Their scientific name *Garrulus glandarius* translates as 'chatterer of acorns', which roughly describes this bird's main function as a noisy hunter-gatherer.

EURASIAN MAGPIE

FAMILY: *Corvidae*

DISTRIBUTION: Found throughout Europe, Asia and much of northwest Africa

HABITAT: Often seen in open areas, particularly farmland, woodland, towns and gardens

Magically monochrome but with a hint of the metallic about its wing feathers, the beautifully bold magpie is a prime example of avian confidence. It evolved from a crow-like bird that existed 17 million years ago. Fossils dating back 20 million years have been found in Europe and Asia, which support the theory that magpies have a long and colourful history throughout the world. Today it is estimated there are eighteen different species of magpies, from the black billed and Oriental magpie – neither one that dissimilar to the Eurasian in hue – to the more vibrant Sri Lankan blue, or Javan green varieties.

One thing they all have in common is their intelligence, and an innate curiosity which is often piqued by human interaction. They are friendly birds with a tendency to seize the day – and their next meal. Whether that is a tasty grub tunnelling beneath the surface of the soil, a tick upon a cow's rump or the farmer's left-out grain, all is fair when it comes to sourcing food. Magpies are opportunists, always on the lookout for a morsel or foodie treat to swipe. That said, there is a softer, more romantic side to this bird.

Once it has chosen and wooed its mate, the magpie will stay true and devoted to the end, and should a male die while the female still has eggs in the nest, a new male will step up to raise and protect the little ones despite the lack of biological connection. This selfless devotion is quite different from the skewed belief that magpies are evil and in cahoots with the devil, a theory that was prevalent during the Victorian era. In Europe at that time there were many superstitions linked to this bird, but ancient history has an alternate view.

The Romans believed the magpie was lucky, and quickly noted its intelligence, attributing this gift to the sun god Apollo. The bird was linked to this deity, and thought to have magical powers and the ability to see the future. In ancient Greece this bird was associated with the god of wine and pleasure Dionysus. In the Far East the magpie is synonymous with good fortune – should you hear one sing, you will be blessed with an abundance of happiness, while the Native Americans noted the bird's bravery and associated it with fearlessness, which is why some tribes wore magpie feathers as they went into battle.

As Christianity spread throughout the world, so too did an abundance of superstitions and narratives that marred the magpie's reputation. Stories of the bird's unfaithfulness, particularly at the time of the crucifixion of Christ, were rife. It was thought that the magpie was the only bird not to weep or to offer comfort to Jesus during his ordeal. This belief was likely down to its pied appearance, which was considered evil at the time. In the nineteenth century, a deviation of the biblical tale of Noah spread by word of mouth. It claimed that the magpie was the only bird who refused to enter the Ark. Other tales suggested the magpie was a strange hybrid of a raven and a dove, and not officially baptized by the church. One of the most common superstitions that started as a rumour and spread quickly was the idea that this bird carried a drop of the devil's blood in its tongue. Should you cut the tongue in two and release the blood, then the magpie would be able to speak like a human.

The sight of magpies in groups, pairs or on their own also gave rise to the popular rhyme which begins 'One for sorrow, Two for joy...', with a list of regional variations throughout the UK. While most believe that the sight of a solitary bird is a bad omen, in truth the misfortune is the magpie's, because it is likely they have lost a mate. To counteract the sadness, you should salute the bird or offer a cheery greeting to turn the luck around for both of you.

The original version of the popular magpie rhyme, which started as a four-line verse:

> One for sorrow,
> Two for mirth,
> Three for a funeral,
> Four for a birth

can be traced back to the sixteenth century, and was first recorded by John Brand in 1777.

◆

A popular superstition in France claims that evil nuns are reincarnated as magpies.

◆

Contrary to popular belief, magpies do not like glittery things. They are scared of them, and so farmers often place shiny objects in their fields to keep them away from their crops.

◆

A group of magpies is called a 'parliament', but they are also known as a 'gulp', 'tribe' or 'tiding'.

SONGBIRDS

As the seasons shift and the harsh frost of winter is met with spring's tender kiss, there is a gentle movement in the air. Something is stirring, picking through the dew-damp grass, looking for morsels to fill a hungry stomach. As if to announce the turn of wheel, it lifts an oil-black head and begins to sing an aria that rings with truth. The blackbird cannot be ignored when it is in full song, and it is not on its own. Songbirds come into full glory with the return of the sun, from the merry soaring of the skylark as it delves into its mighty repartee to the rich and melodious notes of the nightingale, hiding its light in a bushel and blending into the undergrowth. The dawn chorus is a special kind of magic delivered by many of the feathered songsters that you will find in this chapter. Whether they sing morning or night, they all have one thing in common: the ability to spread joy and beauty throughout the world.

EURASIAN SKYLARK

FAMILY: *Alaudidae*

DISTRIBUTION: Found in Europe, Asia and North Africa

HABITAT: Farmland, grassland, meadows, moorland, marshes and wetlands

Sweet and joyful, the tuneful descant of the skylark has touched many hearts over the years. While it may be small in stature, its gift for music is apparent to anyone who has strolled through golden fields during the summer months. That said, this bird will sing at almost any time of year, although it has a preference for sunny days and early morning performances.

Usually one of the first birds to raise its voice during the dawn chorus, the gifted male will use his remarkable song to express a range of emotions. Rising almost vertically from the ground, sometimes up to heights of around 300 m (985 ft), the ardent male hovers for several minutes while singing a beautiful aria to woo the female. This 'flight song' is one of the most distinctive features of the bird, which is an Old World species of lark. The louder and more varied the performance, the more likely it is that he will win over his audience and attract a mate. He also uses his singing voice to assert aggression and let other males know that this is his territory.

This little bird has drawn the attention of poets, artists and writers. Percy Bysshe Shelley, considered one of the greatest English poets of the Romantic era, immortalized its vibrant song in his poem 'To a Skylark' (1820). Here he praises the bird's uplifting song, attributing it with the purity of happiness. Chaucer, too, was a fan, referring to it in his narrative 'The Knight's Tale' (c. 1386), as 'the bisy lark, messenger of the day'. The famous composer Ralph Vaughan Williams was equally captivated by the skylark's offerings, and reimagined them in the musical work 'The Lark Ascending' (1914/20) which was based on a poem of the same name penned by George Meredith in 1881.

When the Skylark is not singing at the top of its voice, it spends its time foraging in arable fields and meadows in search of grain, seeds and other tasty titbits. Plant shoots, leaves and insects are also a part of the diet, especially during autumn and winter, when grain crops are sparse. These small birds like the freedom of open spaces and grassland, so that they have a clear view of any predators. Just as well, as skylarks are prone to attack from falcons, jays, snakes and foxes. The chicks in particular are vulnerable, as skylarks nest in hollows upon the ground, usually in patches of short grass, which means the babies are easily exposed. To make up for the shortfall in predated chicks, these birds tend to have three broods each season, laying three to four eggs each time.

A symbol of hope and joy around the world, the skylark is treasured in many mythologies. The ancient Greeks associated the bird's sweet song with their goddess Hera. It was thought that the beautiful melody it produced epitomized the love between Zeus and his queen, and that Hera blessed the lark with immortality. Ostara, the Germanic goddess of the dawn (also known as Eostre), was deeply saddened when she came upon a frozen lark one morning in early spring. Almost dead, the tiny bird's wings were damaged by the icy cold, and while the goddess could not save it as it was, she took it in her hands and with a warm breath transformed it into a hare. In return, the newly changed creature gifted the goddess with eggs, and so the link between Easter and eggs was established, and the lark became synonymous with hope, renewal and the spring.

The ancient Egyptians associated the bird with their mother goddess Isis, making it a popular emblem of fertility and new life. Its link to the brighter, lighter days of summer would have fuelled this idea, as the bird seemed to spring to life beneath the light of the sun. To this day, many cultures around the world believe that the song of the skylark is a sign of good things to come, and as those who are lucky enough to hear and see its magical 'flight song' will attest, it is one of nature's finest blessings.

Skylark melodies usually last up to several minutes and contain between 160 and 460 syllables. The longest skylark song recorded was approximately 30 minutes in length, while the entire process of taking flight, performing and then returning to the ground can take around an hour to complete.

♦

The collective noun for a group of skylarks is an 'exultation'. They have also been called a 'descent' and a 'bevy'.

♦

Lark shooting was a popular sport in Victorian England. If the birds managed to escape this fate, they were at risk of being caught and kept in cages as songbirds. While most countries have outlawed this practice, shooting larks is still a popular sport in France.

♦

The cottage garden bloom larkspur was named after the bird, because its petals and calyx resemble the lark's sharp rear claw.

EUROPEAN GOLDFINCH

FAMILY: *Fringillidae*

DISTRIBUTION: Widely distributed throughout Europe, the British Isles, Africa and parts of Asia, and introduced to other countries including Australia, New Zealand and Uruguay

HABITAT: Orchards, parks, gardens, woodlands, thickets, heaths, farmland and meadows

Native to Europe, North Africa and Western and Central Asia, the Eurasian goldfinch, which has fourteen different subspecies and belongs to the same family as the canary, has been a fixture for many years. Its name gives us a clue to its longstanding origins. 'Goldfinch' features in many ancient Anglo-Saxon texts, although it has been gifted a variety of names over the years, including 'Goldspink', 'Gold linnet' and 'King Harry'. The Latin moniker *Carduelis carduelis* is formed from the Latin word for thistle, 'carduus', and the bird was known as the thistle finch, because of its love of the plant's seeds. It is this proclivity that has led to the unusually pointed beak of this finch, which helps the bird source upon these tasty treats. Often called a 'charm of goldfinch' when seen in groups, this description hails from the fifteenth-century Anglo-Saxon phrase, 'a chyrme of fynches'.

Associated with money thanks to its striking gold plumage, the Tudors adopted the term 'goldfinch' for a collection of coins, and men of wealth were often referred to as 'goldfinches'. This gave birth to a curious superstition that claimed if an unmarried woman saw a goldfinch on Valentine's Day, she would meet and marry a man of substance.

During the nineteenth century, it was popular practice to cage the bird and keep it as a pet, and scientists soon discovered that this could have an effect on the finch's general appearance. Goldfinches kept in complete darkness lost all the colour from their plumage, turning jet black from head to toe. That said, most socialites preferred to keep their birds happy, well-fed and in the light to retain the vibrant good looks associated with the species. Reports attest that birds kept in this way seemed to thrive, with some living well into their twentieth year. With their beautiful song and natural aptitude for learning, the goldfinch became a popular parlour performer, and was known for its ability to carry out tricks liking ringing a bell, pulling a cart or even playing dead to amuse its human audience.

In art, the bird is often depicted in the hands of Christ as a young child or in the company of the Virgin Mary. Its presence in such Renaissance portraits gives it a strong link to religion, and in particular the Christian faith. It is thought that the bird got its red cap when it pulled a thorn from Christ's brow during the crucifixion. A few drops of blood splashed on its head, and this is how it attained its rosy glow. This myth is often attributed to the robin, too, with a similar story claiming this is the reason for the bird's red breast. Considered sacred because of its links to Christianity, the goldfinch symbolizes the strength to rise above earthly struggles and thrive in testing times.

Commonly seen as a fortuitous omen, particularly if it visits your home and garden, the goldfinch is praised for its sunshine brightness and enchanting song. The Celts associated this bird with the fey, believing the golden streak of light that danced amongst the trees had fairy origins, and its Irish name, lasair choille (flame of the forest), accentuates this idea. To the ancient Greeks the goldfinch was a symbol of joy and beauty associated with Aphrodite the goddess of love, and also Apollo, the vibrant sun god. The Native Americans believed this bird to be synonymous with celebration and positivity, seeing one as an omen of good things to come, making it a sign of hope. In Chinese mythology this joyful finch was a symbol of protection and healing. This idea that the bird could remove all ills was popular in Europe during the medieval period. It was thought that you should carry the bird into the room of a sick person. If the finch's gaze fell away from the person, they would likely die of their affliction, but if the bird fixed its stare upon them, they would be healed.

After mating, all goldfinches will moult, and this tends to affect the brightness of their plumage. The American goldfinch is the only member of the finch family that moults twice a year. Over winter it has drab brown feathers, while in the summer it returns to its usual bright yellow plumage with a black cap.

♦

European goldfinches are highly sociable and like hanging out in groups. They communicate with each other through their high-pitched tinkling songs which include trills, twitters and a persistent 'teLLIT, teLLIT, teLLIT' call.

♦

Female goldfinches are house-proud. Their cup-shaped nests, which are comprised of moss and lichen and then lined inside with wool, are often decorated with little flowers.

CUCKOO

FAMILY: *Cuculidae*

DISTRIBUTION: Cuckoos can be found on every continent except
Antarctica

HABITAT: Woodland areas, farmland, heathland, moors, meadows
and reed beds

A migrating bird, the cuckoo visits the UK every spring, travelling from its winter home of Africa to roost and breed. When summer arrives in early June, it is off again, back to the warmth of the African sun. Young birds will follow in the wake of the adults a few months later, but those still in the nest usually take a full year to make this flight.

Typically dark grey in plumage, this medium-sized bird is often mistaken for a kestrel or sparrowhawk in flight because of its slender body, but can be distinguished by the deviation of its tail which is graduated in appearance. With a bright yellow ring around the eyes and a downward curved beak which resembles a bird of prey, the cuckoo, which is a brood parasite, uses what it has to gain access to a host nest. Sometimes it waits for the nest owner to leave, and sometimes it scares the bird away, depending on the urgency of its need. Once clear, the bird will remove, or even eat, one of the host's eggs, then replace it with one of its own. While some birds are savvy to the intrusion and will attack or defend their home, most do not notice the changeling egg, as it is disguised to look exactly like their own.

While cuckoos have the pick of hosts to parasitize, and have used a number of different species, they mainly approach dunnocks, meadow pipits, reed warblers and pied wagtails.

Black caps are also favourites, but this species is less likely to succumb to the deception, having grown accustomed to the cuckoo's wily tricks. Each female has her preference based on a genetic predisposition and the influence of her own foster parents. If, for example, she was raised by dunnocks, then it is likely she will seek out a dunnock host for her own chick. The bogus egg fits in nicely with the brood, but once hatched will surreptitiously murder each of the other chicks. Going by instinct, it rolls the remaining eggs over the edge of the nest or topples older hatchlings over the side while the mother remains clueless to the traitor in her midst. Even as the chick gets bigger, its foster parents are oblivious, thanks to the bird's ability to mimic the sounds of the other babies. The plaintiff calls it makes are enough to secure the undivided attention of each parent, and an ample supply of food.

With its cunning reputation, the cuckoo is the ideal bird to represent trickery and transformation, and many mythologies latched on to this idea in stories and folklore. The father of the Greek gods, Zeus, did his best to woo the goddess Hera, but his courtship failed. In a last attempt to win her heart he changed into a cuckoo. The small and somewhat dishevelled appearance of the bird struck a chord with the goddess, and she immediately covered it with her cloak, keeping it warm and well-fed, treating it like a pet. Eventually Zeus revealed his true identity and the two were wed, although theirs was a particularly rocky union. Even so, the bird became a symbol of marriage to the ancient Greeks, and a sign of renewed hope thanks to its link with spring.

The Celts associated this winged wonder with the cycles of life. Synonymous with death, rebirth and the coming of spring, the cuckoo's call was seen as a positive omen. In Europe, the bird was commonly associated with insanity, and people were called 'cuckoos' when they had lost their minds. It is thought that the term originated from the phrase 'cloud cuckoo land' which was used to describe a fantasy land or state of being in the play The Birds (c. 414 B.C.), by Aristophanes. Similarly, the term 'cuckold' which is used to belittle the husband of a cheating wife, comes from the French word, 'coucou', for 'cuckoo'. It likens the adulterous wife, who lays in another man's bed, to the devious cuckoo who lays her eggs in another bird's nest.

The cuckoo is one of the only birds that is named for its distinctive call around the world. In Holland it is called the 'koekoek', in Germany the 'kuckuk', in Russia the 'kukush-ka' and in Japan the 'kak-kō'.

♦

In Sweden, there is a strange superstition about the bird's call. If it comes from the direction of the west it symbolizes good luck, if it comes from the east it represents consolidation, if it comes from the south it is an omen of death and if it comes from the north, it is synonymous with sorrow.

♦

The famous cuckoo clock, which gets its name from this bird and usually features the appearance of a cuckoo to mark the hour, hails from the Black Forest in Germany.

BLUE TIT

FAMILY: *Paridae*

DISTRIBUTION: Widespread throughout Europe (except Iceland and
northern parts of Scandinavia), the British Isles and in
parts of the Middle East

HABITAT: Deciduous woodland, parks, gardens and scrub

This colourful bird has a playful demeanour and can be
seen feasting at bird tables and feeders, and flitting from
bush to tree. With its striking colourways of sulphur yellow
breast, bluey-green wing feathers and black and white facial
markings, it adds a much-needed splash of vibrance to the
view, particularly on dull spring mornings – no wonder it is
associated with joy!

Native to Europe, the first recorded sightings of the blue tit
predate the sixteenth century, but the Latin name goes some
way to reveal the bird's ancient origins. It was first called the
Parus caeruleus by the Swedish biologist and physician Carl
Linnaeus, with the word 'caeruleus' meaning 'dark blue' in
Latin, a nod to the bird's cap and wing feathers. This was
recently changed to *Cyanistes caeruleus*, which means 'dark
blue, dark blue'. This comes from the Greek word 'kuanos'
meaning 'dark blue', but while the Greek and Latin names
accentuate the hue of the bird, the 'tit' bit picks up on its
miniscule size. The Old English word 'titmose', meaning
'small bird', dates back to the fourteenth century and was the
original title for this bird, originating from the Old Norse
word 'tit' meaning 'tiny creature' and 'mase' which translates
as 'small bird'. Over time the name evolved into 'titmouse'
and by the sixteenth century blue tits were known by this

moniker. Eventually the name was shortened to 'tit' and the 'blue' bit was added to distinguish the species.

Interestingly, the blue tit has acquired a number of nicknames over the years, including 'Tom tit', 'blue bonnet', and 'blue ox-eye'. 'Nun' was another popular choice, thanks to the blue and white plumage which resembled a nun's garb. Another was 'Billy biter', a reference to the fact that blue tits defend their nest fiercely, and have been known to hiss and nip at fingers should anyone attempt to steal their eggs. This kind of behaviour is not surprising when you consider that the female usually produces one brood, and so each creamy white freckled egg is of great importance. Laying anything from seven to nineteen eggs each time, she is the sole incubator of her young, a process which lasts up to two weeks. Even so, the male does pull his weight, sustaining the female during this time with regular meals and doing most of the active feeding when the chicks are hatched. The newly born chicks fledge at around eighteen days, and after four weeks will be completely self-sufficient.

Recognized as a symbol of happiness and positivity around the world, many cultures believe that seeing the bird is an omen of good fortune. In the Far East the blue tit is a prominent feature in artwork, possibly because of its vivid plumage, but its petite charm and playful character also have a part to play. It has an important role in the afterlife according to Chinese folklore. Acting as a spiritual guide, tales abound of blue tits accompanying the spirits of the dead to the next life. The Celts believed the bird was lucky, and an aid to healing. Its cheery song could be heard throughout the summer and so it became synonymous with the warmth of the sun.

Fans of the blue tit will know of its curious nature, which means it is likely to enter homes and out-buildings, or nest in roofs, in its search for somewhere safe to roost. While some might see this as an inconvenience, it is considered highly fortuitous for any humans within the vicinity. Folklore attests that the bird is a lucky charm and also has protective qualities, especially when it comes to hearth and home. There are superstitions that claim its song is a sign of bad weather to come, but a little wind and rain is a small price to pay.

One of the most efficient and effective pest killers amongst the bird realm, the blue tit is a voracious hunter with a huge appetite.

♦

Blue tits are naturally inquisitive and will watch other birds of the same species and copy what they are doing. This unique behaviour led to a strange phenomenon in the 1920s, when British blue tits began to peck open bottle tops to get to the cream at the top. This behaviour was passed from generation to generation, by copying each other!

♦

Egg hatching is a finely tuned process timed to coincide with the buds bursting on the trees, particularly oak trees. This careful planning means there is always an abundance of caterpillar prey for the young chicks to feed on.

♦

Male blue tits create special songs for a range of purposes. The melodies can warn other male birds off their territory, act as an alarm or attract a potential mate.

WOODPECKER

FAMILY: *Picidae*

DISTRIBUTION: Almost worldwide, apart from Australasia and New Guinea

HABITAT: Woodlands, scrublands, forest, parks and sometimes gardens

Diverse and quirky, the woodpecker is a clever species that has adapted over the ages to fill a niche in the avian kingdom. Most likely this enigmatic bird originated in Eurasia. The discovery of a leg-bone fossil in Germany from around 25 million years ago substantiates this.

Whatever the history, the prehistoric woodpecker soon realized that the tastiest grubs could be found beneath the surface of wood, and so the chisel-like beak came into action, allowing this nifty bird to secure a plentiful source of nourishment. Over time it adapted, developing a stronger skull, neck and bill so that it could drill successfully and carve out a nest in the wood, followed by strong agile feet and rigid tail feathers which helped it to grip the trunk and balance. With these skills the woodpecker flourished, showing a flair for navigating rough, rotten tree bark and also using its super-sturdy beak as a home-building hammer and a tool for communication.

Today there are approximately 300 species around the world. Most of these share flamboyant black and white markings around the head and tail feathers, along with splashes of red and yellow in the plumage. That said, there are many variations and woodpeckers come in other patterns and colourways, with some displaying greenish tinted wings.

Mostly solitary, these birds prefer to go it alone or travel in pairs. They are also surprisingly quiet for most of the year, except in spring when you can hear a loud laughing call followed by the drumming of the beak against the trees. This is the male of the species establishing its territory during the breeding season, and also doing his best to attract a potential mate.

The genus Picus, which comes from the Latin word meaning 'woodpecker', appears in Roman mythology. Picus was widely recognized as an agricultural deity, while also being a feathery tree-dwelling creature and a common sight in forests. Sacred to the god of war Mars, this was no doubt a nod to the ferocious drilling beak which gave this bird an edge. It must have appeared aggressive to the ancients, and well matched to this dynamic deity. An important bird to the Romans, the woodpecker was rarely eaten because of its link to Mars. Instead, people would look to the bird to divine the future, and even carry its beak as a powerful and protective charm. Also associated with herbs and plants from the Paeonia family, which were commonly used for digestive problems, it was thought that these should only be harvested during the night for fear that the woodpecker would see and peck out the eyes of the perpetrator.

Over time, Picus changed from a deity to an early king of Italy, thanks to some imaginative storytelling. This unfortunate soul, who was also the son of the god Saturn, was transformed into a woodpecker by the sorceress Circe. In Norse mythology the woodpecker was linked to the god of thunder Thor. It was thought that its noisy drilling was akin to the god wielding his hammer Mjölnir. To the Celts this bird was an omen of bad weather, and its shrill screeching call was a sign of a storm to come. This is a common theme around the world: in France the green woodpecker was also called the 'rain bird'.

Most often the woodpecker is seen as a symbol of sacred knowledge, and many Celtic and Native American tribes believed this charming bird had the magical ability to traverse the spiritual realms. The predominant theme of the beliefs that surround this bird is persistence when seeking out hidden treasure, making the woodpecker a popular totem for those with a goal in mind.

Not all woodpeckers live in forests. The Gila woodpecker lives in the southwestern desert of North America and drills holes in cacti.

♦

Their tongues are so long they can wrap around the skull, and once flexed acts like a seat belt anchoring the skull and spine during wood drilling.

♦

Acorn woodpeckers plan ahead by caching nuts in tree holes during the winter months.

♦

Woodpeckers have parrot-like feet. Known as zygodactyl, each foot has two toes pointing forwards and two pointing backwards. This gives them a secure grip and allows them to circumnavigate tree trunks safely.

ROBIN

FAMILY: *Muscicapidae*
DISTRIBUTION: Most of Europe, North Africa and Central Asia
HABITAT: Forests, hedges, parks and gardens

This small but feisty bird is a favourite of many. Robins famously feed from the hand once trust has been established. That said, they can be aggressive where other birds are concerned, vigorously warning them off their territory and challenging them in a flurry of feathers and loud noises. Their song is a part of their armoury, and while they will call out in alarm and to attract a mate, they like to give voice at almost any hour, being one of the first birds to join the dawn chorus and one of the last to finish whistling at night.

The males work hard when it comes to courtship. Their energy and bravado serve them well, and they can be heard singing from early spring to secure a mate, with some impatient souls beginning to woo as early as January. Once they have found a potential female, they will endeavour to win her heart with tasty treats which she politely begs for by quivering her wings. The foodie gifts cement the bond between the two, and when the pairing is ready to couple up, the female will begin to build the nest. Interestingly, robins are known to make quirky choices when it comes to their nest site, using old pots, pans and kettles, and venturing into sheds and other buildings. Most commonly they nest in bushes, tree hollows or log piles. They prefer to be close to the ground and in a tightly packed space, cocooned for safety.

Robins usually have four to six eggs per brood, and the female will incubate them while the male keeps her well-fed and nurtured. Once the chicks have hatched, both birds take turns in feeding them until they are ready to fledge. Young robins, though similar in shape and form to the adults, are golden brown in hue and speckled, only attaining their rosy red breasts after a couple of months.

While robins tend to remain resident in their country of birth, some do migrate. Usually, it is the female that takes this journey, flying from British shores to enjoy some winter sunshine in southern Europe. Scandinavian robins will flee to Britain and western Europe during the turn of the seasons. All migrating birds return to their usual breeding grounds in the spring to couple up, but while the location is the same, the mate will often be new.

The robin's enduring relationship with humankind is timeless and tales abound of how this little charmer won its scarlet breast. Interestingly, it was always known as the 'redbreast' before the addition of the name robin was added as a prefix, thanks to a European custom of attributing names to birds. Christian folklore attests that it was an act of kindness that caused the robin's colour change. The bird decided to fan the flames of the fire to keep baby Jesus warm as he slept in his manger but it flew too close. The embers tarnished its chest feathers turning them bright red. In other tales it was the robin who gently teased the thorns from Christ's brow whilst he was on the cross, and a speck of blood tainted its breast and face.

To Norse people, the robin was associated with their god of thunder Thor, and had the power to protect those early tribes from lightning bolts, while the Celts were enamoured with the robin's beauty, believing it represented the birth of the new sun during the winter solstice. Its colourful breast and song were a testament to the returning light, and the hope and joy that came with it. In Irish folklore the bird was considered a bad omen, especially if it entered the home where it became a portend of death. If one happened to die in the palm your hand, then you would suffer a tremor in that hand for the rest of your life.

The Victorians really fell for the robin's merits. Not only was it a cheerful and confident bird, happy to sing for its human audience, but it became synonymous with Christmas, thanks to posties sporting a bright red uniform while delivering festive cards and gifts. They were affectionately called 'robins', and the bird was forever tied to the season of goodwill, featuring on cards and decorations.

There are numerous collective nouns to describe a group of robins. 'Round' is the most common, but they can also be called a 'breast', 'blush', 'rabble', 'bobbin', 'riot' and 'hood'.

◆

Robin skins were popular adornments for ladies' hats at the end of the Victorian era.

◆

Every continent has a species of robin, but only the Japanese and Ryukyu robins are related to the European version. The American robin, which was named after the European robin because of its red breast, is actually a type of thrush.

◆

Robins have a sweet tooth. While their usual diet is insects and worms, they also eat fruit, seeds and nuts, and have been known to tuck into cakes and pastries.

SWALLOW

FAMILY: *Hirundinidae*

DISTRIBUTION: Europe, Asia, Africa and the Americas

HABITAT: Farmland, wetland, grassland and buildings near rivers or lakes

The darting sight of this diminutive songbird is one of the joys of spring. Slender in body and wing, with a long, pointy, sometimes deeply forked tail and a tiny bill, the swallow is a streak of oily blue, scooting at top speed along the edge of the breeze. Like its contemporaries the swift and the nightjar, the swallow has a strong, wide jaw that makes it easy to snaffle in-flight snacks.

These hole nesters were thought to have originated in Africa and then spread across to Europe where they found ample supplies and homesteads to nest in during the summer months. Today the birds undertake the epic 6,000-mile journey from UK shores to South Africa twice a year; leaving in late September to winter in Cape Province, then returning in the spring to enjoy a British summer.

While they are called swallows, this is a general term for the more specific breed, the barn swallow. The name itself comes from the old English term 'swell' meaning to swirl, and was attributed because of the bird's smooth, swooping flight. The Norse word swala, which means 'cleft stick', could also have some influence and be a reference to the swallow's lengthy tail.

Belonging to the songbird family *Hirundinidae*, which also includes martins and comprises of around ninety species worldwide, the swallow's population has swelled over the years, thanks to the introduction of agriculture and farming. These industrious birds like to nest near cattle for the constant heat they produce, which provides the ideal environment for chicks to hatch and fledge. There is also the added bonus of a ready supply of insects to feast upon. Both male and female birds play their part in building the nest using a mixture of mud, grass and saliva to form handy pellets which they use to build up the sides. Once the basic nest is in place, they will carefully line it with grass and then feathers. This entire process can take anything from a week to twenty-three days, but these birds are precise for a reason. They will often re-use the same nest the following year, so they need it to be secure and hardy to withstand the passing of time. Swallows also know the benefit of teamwork, often congregating at night in small flocks to keep predators at bay. They will mob unsuspecting birds of prey or intruders that happen to invade their territory, and the male will ardently defend his nest, often toppling other males by grabbing their feet in flight and dragging them to the ground.

Being fleet of wing and seeming to glide gracefully through the ether, it is no surprise that swallows have a close connection with the gods. In Chinese mythology, these nifty birds were thought to have been born from the tears of the gods. As such, they were positive omens, commonly used on coins and seals to illustrate divine protection. In Asia and Eastern Europe, it was thought that swallows were responsible for bringing fire from the deities to the people. Their role as heavenly emissaries was common in many cultures, and in Africa it was believed that they were long dead ancestors, returned to Earth as birds to watch over and protect the living. In Russian mythology, it was thought that swallows were the spirits of dead children returned in feathered form, while the Greeks believed they were symbols of fortune, and often kept live birds in the home to attract good luck. The Japanese liked to mark the day the swallows returned to roost. They offered gifts and treats to the birds as a way of ensuring fertility within the family home. Some people still celebrate the return of these hardy birds, welcoming them with open arms and barns, believing their presence alone will protect their property from flood, storm and lightning.

According to Christian legend, a small group of swallows did their best to lead the soldiers away from the Gardens of Gethsemane when they came to take Jesus to his death.

♦

Sailors love swallows. According to seafaring folklore, they are a positive omen for those travelling over water. Sailors would ink the image of this bird upon their body as a good luck charm.

♦

Swallows do almost everything on the wing. They eat and drink on the wing, swooping close to the water to take a swig. They also bathe on the wing, scooting against the water for a quick sluice during flight.

NIGHTINGALE

FAMILY: *Muscicapidae*

DISTRIBUTION: Found in southern Europe and western Asia, these birds migrate to central Africa during the winter months

HABITAT: Favouring dense vegetation, they are usually found in woodland and forests, hiding in bushes or thick scrub

While it is known for its musical talents, particularly at night, it is only the male nightingale that sings during the breeding season. The low, rich notes it produces are a simple song of love and a way of advertising the bird's paternal skills to attract a mate. It is thought that the most gifted performers will show more care to their partner, particularly when it comes to feeding and looking after young chicks. Not only that, but deep within the song there is a subtle message which relates the bird's age, strength of immunity and where it comes from, which the female can decipher. With a repertoire of between 180 and 260 song variations, the ardent male has a wealth of material to call upon, but while young males pull out all the stops in their search for love, it is the older males who have a larger, more organized range.

The name 'nightingale' comes from the old English word 'nihtegale' which has been around for at least 1,400 years, and was used as a slang term for someone with a stunning voice. The scientific name *Luscinia megarhynchos* also hints at the bird's amazing talents, for while 'Luscinia' means 'nightingale', 'megarhynchos' comes from two Greek words, 'mega' meaning 'great' and 'rhunkos' meaning 'bill'.

Drab in comparison to other songbirds, the secretive nightingale lacks distinctive markings, being mostly brown with a whitish throat and pale underparts. This means it can easily blend into the undergrowth, making it almost invisible to the eye.

The Romans associated the bird with the goddess Venus, believing that its poignant melodies were filled with love and yearning, and synonymous with the coming of spring. In ancient Persia, the bird was a symbol of unrequited love. Its enchanting symphony was associated with deep longing, as it was it only heard under the shadow of night when restless lovers could not sleep.

Renewal is also at the heart of nightingale symbolism, and the bird was an inspiration to poets and sages, who were deeply moved by its night-time soliloquies. The Greeks attributed this winged wonder with the sombre tale of the princess Philomela. She was the sister of Procne who married King Tereus of Thrace. According to legend, after five years of marriage Procne sent Tereus to Athens to fetch her sister, but when he saw the princess, he was so overcome with lust he raped her. To prevent her from speaking of what he had done, he cut out her tongue. Luckily, Procne discovered the truth of the crime, and after taking her revenge by killing his son and serving him as dinner to the king, Philomela and Procne fled. King Tereus pursued the sisters, swearing to kill them both, but the gods intervened. They turned Procne into a swallow, and the voiceless Philomela into a perfectly formed nightingale. In this guise the princess was able to express herself through song, which she did woefully every evening.

In China, the nightingale is associated with happiness and the rejuvenating power of music. A famous fairy tale claims the little bird had healing powers, after it restored the ailing health of an emperor who once held it captive. According to the tale, the emperor was so enamoured by its song he had it captured and caged, but when the gift of a mechanical bird appeared he lost interest in the real thing. The nightingale returned to the woods while the emperor played with his new toy, but when he fell ill the repetitive melody of the fake bird did nothing to restore his spirits. As he slipped into a stupor the faint chirruping of the nightingale's song could be heard, as the faithful bird returned to his bedside. The tune it sang filled the emperor with such hope that he instantly felt better, and so the bird was swiftly recognized as a symbol of rebirth and joy.

While the most notable feature of their song is the haunting crescendo, nightingales also make 'frog-like' noises when they are disturbed. These alarming calls are at odds with the usual beautiful melodies they produce.

♦

The males keep trim by singing! They lose weight with each nightly performance, as it takes so much energy to produce and maintain their song.

♦

The nightingale is the national bird of Ukraine. According to legend, when the bird first visited the country, it was so struck by all the sad songs of the people that it puffed out its chest and serenaded them with a joyful melody. From that moment on the people sang happier tunes and the bird returned each spring to hear them.

HOUSE SPARROW

FAMILY: *Passeridae*

DISTRIBUTION: Worldwide distribution, except the North and South Poles, native to Eurasia and North Africa

HABITAT: Urban and suburban areas, gardens and farmland, found in homes nesting in eaves and outbuildings

The sparrow may seem dull to some, but its story is one of epic proportions. This enterprising bird has managed to succeed by cleverly intertwining its fate with that of humankind. There are many who see this small brown bird as a pest, while others have grown fond of its perky charms.

The male of the species is the most striking, having streaky chestnut brown wings with a grey head cap and undersides, and a black bib. The female is pale brown all over with buff undersides, but what she lacks in colour she makes up for in industry, raising two or three broods of chicks a year. That said, there is more to this success story than meets the eye. Sparrows may be common; found in North and South America, Europe, Australasia, and Asia – but it hasn't always been this way and the bird's numbers ebb and flow yearly.

The jaw bones of a house sparrow, or something very similar, were found buried in a cave in Israel, and thought to be at least 100,000 years old. Also discovered in the same caves were remnants of humans, which suggest that even in those early times this bird knew that interaction with people was necessary for its survival. Roll forward to around 20,000 years ago, and more fossil records surface of birds that resemble sparrows, again in Israel. It is clear from the discoveries that the numbers had increased, thanks to living alongside humans and capitalizing on the scraps, grain and other commodities on offer.

As agriculture developed, the species spread across the continent to Europe and these new birds evolved into different types of sparrows, depending on where they lived. With a canny knack for adapting to their environment and having an opportunistic nature, they made themselves at home, in our homes. Nesting in roofs and out-buildings, and helping themselves to any titbits that we had no need for, they took what they could find and upcycled it! They also made good work of any home-grown crops, which is how their controversial reputation began.

With all this food in plentiful supply, it is no wonder there was an abundance of sparrows around the world, giving rise to a movement in Europe during the 1700s to exterminate the species. In Russia, they even lowered taxes depending on the number of the birds' heads you could provide. While this must have been incentive for many, sparrows still had their fans, but the numbers were dwindling fast. The fate of the bird fluctuated. The colourful history of the sparrow goes some way to explain its appeal. This is a resilient bird that has learnt to bide its time and also seize the moment when prime pickings are on offer. It is no surprise then that it features in mythologies around the world as a symbol of love and good fortune. The ancient Egyptians prized the sparrow for its intelligence, and would often keep the bird caged to enhance the keeper's inner wisdom. To them it was a symbol of hope and rebirth. The Greeks associated the sparrow with their goddess of love Aphrodite, believing that it was synonymous with passion, loyalty and enduring love. It even gets a mention in the Bible, where the true worth of this small bird is given prominence in the quote 'are not two sparrows sold for a penny?'

Whatever the secret is, the sparrow is a versatile bird with plenty of merits and a wealth of history, which goes to prove that it may be common in numbers but in every other way it is far from ordinary.

A Scottish legend tells the tale of a group of sparrows who help a man to build his house on the understanding that he leaves a hole in the roof where they can roost. The birds live in the man's home undisturbed and in return bring him much good fortune.

◆

In Turkey, it is common to refer to your little or pinkie finger as the 'sparrow' finger, as it is small like the bird.

◆

In Australia they use the term 'sparrow's fart' to describe the dawn, or an early part of the day. This slang phrase was first used by country folk in the nineteenth century.

◆

There are approximately 1.6 billion sparrows around the world. Of these, there are forty-three types of Old World sparrows and around 138 New World species.

TURTLE DOVE

FAMILY: *Columbidae*

DISTRIBUTION: Widespread, this migrant breeder can be found in Europe, Central Asia, the Middle East and North Africa

HABITAT: Arable farmland, grassland, heathland, semi-desert environments and forests

Take a stroll between the hedgerows in early summer and you will likely hear the gentle 'purring' of the turtle dove as it ponders the day ahead. This delicate bird may be a pigeon, but there is something distinctly beautiful in the way it holds itself. Pinkish grey in hue, it has monochrome barring upon its neck and mottled brown and black upperparts. Its pink-rimmed eyes stare steadily in the distance, as if sizing up impending threats.

A migratory bird, the turtle dove flees to sunnier climes over winter, travelling as far as Sub-Saharan Africa to get its sunshine fix. A migration of this size is fraught with difficulties. Despite travelling in huge flocks, the birds are hunted and numbers have dwindled significantly over the years. Lack of seed and grain during the breeding season has also had an impact on the population.

Also known as the 'pink bellied turtle dove', and the 'laughing dove', the wild ancestor of the turtle dove is hard to pinpoint, but it has loose associations with the African ringed dove, which was well established in the sixteenth century. Turtle doves are ecologically unique, being the only long-distance migratory dove in Europe. Despite being vulnerable and on the red list of conservation in the UK, these birds do their best to thrive, often having multiple broods per season. That said, their nest-building skills do little for their chance of survival. The nests tend to be flimsy in structure, made from a small gathering of twigs, and usually secreted away in scrub. Being so fragile, they easily break, so the chance of losing eggs is increased; but should a nest collapse, the parents will quickly build a new one, starting the entire process again.

The female usually lays one or two eggs, and both parents take it in turn to incubate them for up to two weeks. Once hatched, the tiny chicks will be fed by crop milk during their first few days. This lumpy pallid substance is secreted from the crop, a thin portion of the digestive tract, and produced by both adults. It has high levels of fat and protein to sustain the newly born chicks. The birds then fledge fully after a couple of weeks.

Most commonly associated with love and romance, thanks to their tender behaviour, the male displays intense emotions when wooing the female. His show of ardour includes expressive vocalizations, head bobbing and puffing out his chest feathers. Once the female's heart is secured, the pairing will last a lifetime, as these birds are famously monogamous and are often seen perched together, preening.

The dove also has a long history in folklore, mythology and the arts, making one of its earliest literary appearances in the 'Song of Solomon'. Here, the bird is a herald of spring, as the flowers return and it can be heard singing. William Shakespeare also included it in a number of his works, such as the poem 'The Phoenix and the Turtle' which was published in 1601. Elizabethan poets and writers were quick to spot the birds' timeless devotion and how they seemed to mourn the loss of their partner, something which North American mourning doves do when they return to the place where they lost their mate. It is thought that even in death they care for their loved one.

Further back in history turtle doves were immortalized, and many ancient civilizations considered them symbols of enduring love. The Roman goddess of trust and good faith Fides was often depicted wearing a laurel wreath crown and white veil while holding the turtle dove lovingly in one hand, to emit a sense of purity. The ancient Greeks also favoured the sweet nature of these birds, and associated them with their goddess of love and beauty Aphrodite. It was thought that a flock of doves pulled her chariot through the skies. The Syrian Astarte, another love goddess linked with purity, was said to have hatched from an egg which was nursed by doves, while the Mesopotamian goddess of love and war Inanna was often accompanied by these birds, no doubt when she was focusing on matters of the heart.

Turtle doves can reveal your love fate. While they are usually considered a symbol of peace, in Europe it is thought that seeing two doves together is a sign you will be blessed with true love.

♦

The ringed turtle dove drinks by sucking water up into its beak. This is a unique skill, as most birds have to tip their head back to drink their fill.

♦

Turtle doves are hardier than they look. During their migration from European shores to Africa, they fly at speeds of up to 97 km/h (60 mph), and can cover stretches of around 700 km (435 miles) without stopping. Most of this flying is done at night.

STARLING

FAMILY: *Sturnidae*

DISTRIBUTION: Native to Europe and parts of Asia and Africa, they have been introduced to North America, South Africa, New Zealand and Australia

HABITAT: Woodland, farmland, parks and gardens

Like slicks of oil pecking their way through the landscape, these iridescent beauties are easy to spot because they come en masse. With dark black wings that have a metallic purple-green sheen in the summer months, and a pretty white flecked pattern in the winter, it is hard to ignore the starling. In truth, this bird is considered a pest by some, hijacking nest cavities carefully prepared by other native birds and spreading disease to livestock. That said, there is much to be admired here, for the starling is a confident and social bird, unafraid of venturing forth into new territory and making waves.

Masters of murmuration, these canny birds have learnt that safety comes in numbers and so they combine their aerial skills in what seems to be a carefully choreographed dance, made up of twists, turns and graceful swooping movements. The manoeuvres they perform create vast shapes which fill the sky at dusk from autumn to spring. One of nature's wonders, this ethereal performance is a clever way of keeping predators at bay. Moving in unison, it is almost impossible to pinpoint a single bird amongst the masses, which serves to confuse hungry kestrels and hawks who might be in the vicinity. Murmurations are always performed above communal roosting grounds, and when the final dip and curve has been demonstrated, the birds will gently alight and settle down for the evening.

To the ancients, these nightly enactments must have seemed divine, and the Romans in particular were entranced by the flock's movements. They looked to the skies for direction, a practice known as 'taking the auspices', and they read the shapes created by the birds, taking inspiration and leadership from them. In truth, daily decisions and politics were hugely influenced by the turn of a starling wing. The Celts, too, recognized the power and potential of this bird, believing them to be messengers from the gods. Their gregarious nature made them less afraid of humans, and the fact they worked together meant they were almost always seen in small noisy groups, scavenging for food.

Starlings are extremely vocal, being distant relatives of myna birds, and they have inherited the same gift of mimicry from their Old World cousins. Both the male and female enjoy singing, although the male is more expressive and will mimic other birds like the jay or meadowlark. They also imitate hawks. It is thought this impressive ability to perfect a range of avian songs makes the male more attractive to the female. The starling's talents do not end there, and there is much debate about its ability to copy the human voice, something that the ancient Greek philosopher Aristotle noted in his works. It is also a quality that Shakespeare admired and made reference to in his play *Henry IV, Part 1*.

It is no surprise that poets, artists and musicians have all been influenced by this charming bird over the years. Its first artistic outing was a mention in the Welsh *Mabinogion*, where it appears as a confidante to the heroine Branwen, who is trapped in an oppressive marriage. Here the bird learns to speak, and then faithfully delivers a message to Branwen's brother, who comes in search of his sister. The great composer and musician Mozart was also a fan, keeping a starling as a pet. He taught the bird to sing many of his famous compositions, and when it died he gave it an elaborate funeral and even penned an elegy in its honour.

While the starling is native to Eurasia, it was introduced to other parts of the world, and according to legend the bird's artistic status played a key role in its foray into North America. In 1890, Eugene Schieffelin of the American Acclimatization Society released a hundred starlings in two groups into New York's Central Park. He cited Shakespeare as his reasoning for this, believing that America should be home to all the birds ever mentioned by the bard. It is thought that this introduction was successful and that all European starlings of America are descendants of these first birds, a theory that still remains in question.

A collection of starlings is known as a 'chattering', 'affliction', 'scourge' or 'constellation'.

♦

Starlings will eat anything from kitchen scraps, worms and bugs to seeds and a variety of berries and fruit – they adapt their diet depending on what is available.

♦

The males usually have dark beaks during the winter, but these will gradually transform into a bright citrus yellow hue in time for the breeding season. The brighter the beak, the healthier the bird.

WREN

FAMILY: *Troglodytidae*

DISTRIBUTION: Found throughout Eurasia and Africa

HABITAT: Heathland, moorland, farmland, hedgerows, gardens, parks, cliffs and rocky areas

Whether tiptoeing through the undergrowth or peeking at a freshy placed feeder, the wren is a small but curious bird with lots of charm. Rotund in appearance, this tiny ball of fluff has a perky upright chestnut tail, long legs and a fine bill, which it combines with a mighty singing voice. Indeed, this little chirruper hardly stops for breath all year round, singing between 500 and 600 notes a minute.

A New World species, meaning it is mostly found in the western hemisphere of North and South America, there is much speculation about this bird's beginnings. It was commonly thought during the twentieth century that wrens were closely related to dippers, mockingbirds and thrushes. The similarities with the dipper's appearance seemed obvious, as they also have rounded wings and a short stumpy build. Both birds tend to favour dome-shaped nests and so conclusions were drawn that led to this belief, but after further DNA research scientists agreed that wrens are more likely related to gnatcatchers, treecreepers and nuthatches.

Whatever their roots, Eurasian wrens, being one of eighty-eight species in the world, are in abundance, living life large despite their diminutive size. They are unique in that they can live in the most diverse habitats, making their homes in woodland, heath, moor, cliff and on the remotest islands. Cracks and crevices are their domain, and they are particularly fond of woodpiles, boulders and fallen trees. Interestingly, their scientific name *Troglodytes troglodytes* means 'cave dweller' and refers to this love of obscure nooks and crannies.

Thriving on tiny morsels of food such as ants, beetles, flies and spiders, wrens have no need to migrate. A bundle of energy, the wren moves swiftly in search of food, and to avoid prying eyes. While it is seldom seen, the male is often heard singing at the top of its voice, swaying from side to side and shaking out its feathers. No wonder it is often referred to in folklore as the 'King of the Birds'.

In truth, the jovial male has much to sing about, thanks to an endless supply of energy and the ability to father broods with different females. Once the first lots of eggs are incubated solely by the first female, he will begin to woo a second, starting the process all over again. If time is in his favour, he may even move on to a third.

Revered throughout Europe, the wren has always had both positive and negative connotations. It was believed that killing one or disturbing its nest would result in bad luck. Throughout Europe the wren was seen as a positive omen. According to legend, when a contest was held to find the King of the Birds, the wren tucked itself tightly within the feathers of the eagle. Because it was shrewd in nature and supposedly as light as feather, the larger bird knew nothing of its presence. As the eagle climbed higher than all of the other birds in the sky, the tiny wren slipped out from beneath its wings and flew above its head, winning the contest and claiming the title for its own.

To the early Christians the wren was a bad omen, as explained by the tale of St Stephen, who took refuge from his persecutors in dense vegetation but was exposed by the noisy bird. Since then, the wren has been tied to St Stephen's

Day which falls on 26 December each year. In parts of Ireland a ritual is re-enacted whereby a fake wren is carried aloft a decorative pole, the idea being that the bird is sacrificed and given back to nature to ensure abundance for the coming year. Up until the twentieth century, real birds were used and given formal funerals. Some communities even had 'Wren Boys' who would dress up and parade around the town, carrying the dead birds, threatening to bury them in people's yards if they did not contribute food or money. While these rites and rituals sound ominous, in truth they were a celebration of the wren's fortuitous nature and a way to honour the cycles of life.

The wren has an abundance of nicknames throughout the world. Most commonly it is called a 'Jenny wren', but it is also known as 'titty', 'titty wren', 'chitty wren', 'tiddly creeper', 'Tom tit' and also 'two fingers', which is thought to be a reference to its small size and tail, which sticks straight up.

♦

Wrens feature in the works of Chaucer, Shakespeare, John Clare, Edward Lear and William Blake, to name a few.

♦

The males pull out all the stops to impress their mate by building several nests and then showing them off. The prospective female usually rejects the first few viewings, before making her final decision based on the safety of the location and proximity to food supply.

BLACKBIRD

FAMILY: *Turdidae*

DISTRIBUTION: Native to Eurasia and North Africa, this bird has also been introduced to Australia, New Zealand and islands that fall within this vicinity

HABITAT: Gardens, woodland and grassland

These joyful birds love to sing during the winter and early spring, especially post-rainfall, giving them the nickname 'stormcock'. When you consider the European blackbird is a 'true thrush' and belongs to the thrush family, then it is no surprise that they are vocally gifted. The rounded head and pointed wings reveal something of its heritage, although the male of the species sports a gleaming black plumage and a citrusy orange-yellow beak. This vibrant accent of colour is matched in the bright yellow that frames its furtive eyes. The female has buff brown feathers and beak, but she is speckled with spots and streaks along the curve of her breast, and is often found in the vicinity of the male.

Evolved from the island thrush of Southeast Asia, the ancestors of the European blackbird likely colonized the Canary Islands, and came to Europe from there. This hardworking bird soon spread, finding ample food and nesting with which to make a home and thrive. Fiercely territorial, these little charmers will protect their patch but tend to go further afield in search of sustenance, which is why you are likely to see them during the winter months when they are active scavengers. During this time the numbers are given a boost by foreign friends. Scandinavian blackbirds, along with Baltic beauties and a few errant German cousins, favour the warmth of British shores and will migrate during the winter, returning in spring for the breeding season.

Most active at dusk and at dawn when they puff out the feathers of their chest and serenade us with a soulful melody, it is no wonder the blackbird was considered spiritual by the Celts, who associated it with the Otherworld. To them, this little creature represented the liminal space between light and dark, and had the ability to cross over into the spiritual realm. The Welsh goddess Rhiannon was closely linked to this bird, and was often depicted with three blackbirds, which were thought to have the power over life and death. The Greeks also thought the bird was magical and held the belief that if it ate pomegranate seeds it would die, suggesting a link to their goddess of the grain Persephone, who had to spend half of the year in the Underworld after eating these seeds.

A popular tale from Irish folklore gives the blackbird kudos for the pivotal role it played in the life of St Kevin of Glendalough, Ireland. Born in A.D. 498, and being a man of good heart and highly religious, Kevin sat in prayer one day in the monastery with his hands held out in front of him. A blackbird flew down and nestled in his palms. Unperturbed, Kevin continued to pray and fell deeper into a spiritual trance, so much so that he failed to notice the bird had begun to build its nest there. Eventually the blackbird laid its eggs, and it was not until the tiny chicks had hatched that Kevin became aware of what had happened. According to folklore, this feat of spiritual dedication was in part responsible for Kevin's sainthood, and from that moment on he was known as the Patron Saint of Blackbirds.

Known as the 'ouzel', 'ousel' or 'wosel' in Old English, the Blackbird is even mentioned in Shakespeare's 'A Midsummer Night's Dream', where the coal-winged beauty is referred to as:

> The Woosell cocke, so blacke of hew,
> With orenge-tawny bill

Widespread, and hugely popular, it claimed the title of the National Bird of Sweden in 1962, and has featured on some of the country's postage stamps.

In folklore, it is thought that if a blackbird nests close to your home, then you will be blessed with an abundance of good fortune.

♦

The average life expectancy of a blackbird is around three to four years, but the oldest blackbird was recorded as living to the princely age of twenty-one years and one month.

♦

Amongst other theories on it is origins, the notorious rhyme:

> Sing a song of sixpence,
> A pocket full of rye,
> Four and twenty blackbirds
> Baked in a pie

was a coded message used by the eighteenth-century pirate Blackbeard to recruit new crew members.

♦

Blackbirds have a beauty regime. They practice 'anting', which means rubbing ants on their feathers to remove parasites and keep their plumage in tip-top condition.

WATERBIRDS

As grey clouds cluster over sandy mudflats and the dampness in the air seeps between skin and bone, the waders gather. Loitering upon the edges, these often-solitary figures haunt the shadows in the dankest, dampest places. Some, like the heron, immerse themselves wholeheartedly into a body of water; stick-thin legs provide scaffolding, holding them aloft as they wade even deeper into the stream. Others, like the duck or the swan, glide seamlessly, going with the flow and navigating both land and watery planes to find the tastiest treats. Downy layers of feather are their only insulation, but it is enough, for they are equipped in other ways. Waterbirds have long been a source of fascination to humankind. From their monogamous ways to the poise with which they hold themselves, they are both ethereal and timeless.

KINGFISHER

FAMILY: *Alcedinidae*

DISTRIBUTION: Found throughout Europe, Asia and North Africa

HABITAT: Usually seen along riverbanks, streams, lakes, ponds and wetland areas

The common kingfisher has mastered the art of invisibility like no other, being inconspicuous despite its vibrant plumage. Spotters will attest to the difficulty of seeing this bird, but it is worth the wait, with its metallic blue back and upperparts and a burnt orange breast, along with an oversized flinty black beak and looming head. Only slightly bigger than a robin but twice the weight, it looks somewhat out of proportion thanks to a sharp lengthy bill.

The earliest kingfisher fossils were discovered in Wyoming, USA, and date back some 30–40 million years, but it is thought that the kingfisher originated in the Indo-Malayan region. Known as the halcyon bird by the ancient Greeks, the species is split into three distinct groups: tree kingfishers, river kingfishers and piscivorous water kingfishers, with around 114 species recorded worldwide.

The stunning plumage of the kingfisher is thanks to the structural make-up of its feathers, and nothing to do with pigment. Known as the Tyndall Effect, tiny dispersed particles within the plumage fragment the light so that it appears in a range of bright blue shades, giving the bird its iridescent gleam.

Gifted with dexterity, these skilful hunters have excellent eyesight and can adjust the way they view things depending on the environment. This makes plunging beneath the surface of the water easy, as their binocular vision means they can judge depth and easily spot their target. The determination they display in catching fish is equalled in the way they guard their nests, which are usually burrowed into riverbanks.

It is no surprise that such a distinctive bird appears in mythology from around the world. The colours of the bird are a prominent feature in many tales, with one biblical narrative claiming that the kingfisher was the first bird that Noah released from the Ark after the great flood. As it rose into the air, the sun hit its underbelly and set its breast aglow with burnished light, while the blue of the sky tinted its back feathers.

To the ancient Greeks this feathered beauty was synonymous with love, and linked to the story of Alcyone and Ceyx. This husband-and-wife duo were madly in love and would refer to each other as the deities Hera and Zeus, which seemed harmless enough, but angered Zeus greatly as it implied that they thought they were just as powerful. When Ceyx, who was King of Trachis, took a journey over water to visit the Oracle at Delphi, there was a terrible storm and a thunderbolt hit his boat. Tales claim this was sent by Zeus in a fit of rage, but either way the boat sank and Ceyx met his doom. When Alcyone discovered that her beloved was dead, she threw herself into the ocean. The gods were so touched by this show of grief that they transformed her into a kingfisher, as they did with Ceyx, and so husband and wife were reunited and known as the halcyon birds. When Alcyone laid her eggs by the shoreline, the winds, which were governed by her father, became calm and placid and the sun shone for a week. This period of time was known as the Halcyon Days and gave birth to the term we recognize today.

The idea that the kingfisher is associated with calm weather was a common belief throughout the world, and the bird was thought to have mystical powers that could control the ebb and flow of the waves. One popular custom in Europe was to carry or wear a kingfisher feather as an amulet for luck. Another strange practice involved preserving the dead bird in its entirety and using it as a moth repellent. More importantly, keeping a dead kingfisher was said to boost abundance, because it was thought that it could renew its plumage even after it had passed on to the next life.

Kingfishers do not like each other much. Their urge to be solitary means that mating can be fraught with tension. The male's mating pose matches its aggressive stance, which can be confusing to female birds.

◆

Kingfisher chicks take it in turns to be fed, using a rotation system. Once the chick at the front has been fed, it moves to the back of the nest to digest its dinner.

◆

The kingfisher's beak was the inspiration for the Japanese bullet train. Engineers copied its construction to prevent sonic boom when the train enters a tunnel.

◆

Kingfishers are blessed with a third, transparent eyelid which comes into use underwater, protecting the surface of the eyes while they are submerged.

DUCK

FAMILY: *Anatidae*

DISTRIBUTION: Found in Europe, Asia and North America, also introduced to South Africa and Australia

HABITAT: Wetland habitats like rivers, lakes, ponds, marshes, as well as wooded swamps and fields, and city parks

According to researchers, a close relative of the duck, known as the 'vegavis', walked alongside dinosaurs more than 65 million years ago. These stealthy birds were thought to have lived in the area which is now present-day Antarctica. Fossils of bones within a deep matrix of rock have been discovered to support this theory, and the lineage leads to the duck we know today. While it is hard to say when ducks were initially domesticated, it is believed that the Egyptians were the first to see the benefits of this bountiful bird, breeding them for food and also using them as sacrifices when petitioning the gods. The Romans, too, were partial to the tender meat of a roasted duck, but would discard the eggs, believing that the white meat was the only thing of value to be had from the bird.

Being both land- and water-dwellers, they have adapted over the years and live happily in groups known as 'paddlings'. These 'on the water' collectives thrive because there is safety in numbers, something which deters most of their predators. With their waterproof feathers, which are coated with a waxy lining to protect the downy inner feathers, and their strong webbed feet, they can swim with ease and also dive to depths of around 73 m (240 ft).

In love, ducks are seasonally monogamous, meaning they stay together during one mating season which can last from four to eight months. While they return to the same breeding ground each year, their romance is left in the hands of fate and they may, or may not, meet up again. In the early stages of their courtship, they will bob heads at each other, which is an initial sign of interest, then the female will decide if the male is suitable by looking at his colourful plumage and size to ascertain whether he could protect her and their eggs.

Ducks are highly prized in different faiths and mythologies. To the Hindus they are sacred birds and associated with the goddess Ganga. This water deity is linked to purification and good fortune, and is often depicted with a giant duck as her mount. The goddess of wealth and abundance, Lakshmi, is also associated with this waterfowl, and sometimes seen with a duck in her hand. In Hungarian mythology, the bird is held in high regard. Being a creature of the earth, the air and the water, it is thought it can transcend the realms, and it even had a part to play in the creation of the world. According to legend, the sun transformed into a duck at the instruction of the 'golden father' and creator god Arany Atyácska. At that time, the planet was covered in water, and it was the duck's role to dive deep beneath the surface and bring back some mud to shape the world. To the ancient Greeks, it was associated with Penelope, the wife of Odysseus. According to the epic tale, when she was born her father Icarus was so disappointed that she was a girl, he cast her into the sea. Luckily a group of ducks carried her to safety. When Icarus saw this, he took it to be a sign from the gods that she was special, and named her Penelope, after the Greek word for 'duck'. The Chinese associated this waterfowl with love and fidelity, taking inspiration from mandarin ducks who develop lasting bonds. They were also synonymous with the idea of kinship and fraternal love, and Oriental poetry transcribed around the third century often compares the brotherly bond with the pairing of these birds.

Ducks never get cold feet, thanks to a bundle of tightly packed blood vessels and arteries which travel down from their legs.

♦

Ducklings communicate while they are in their eggs, by making clicking noises known as 'pipping'. They let each other know when they are going to hatch, so that they can co-ordinate the process. The reason for this is that it is safer to be together. Once hatched they do everything in organized groups, to avoid predation.

♦

Research proves that city ducks make louder, harsher quacks, so that they can be heard above the traffic, while their country cousins produce longer, more relaxed sounds.

♦

Ducks sleep with one eye open, and they also have excellent vision. Their eyes are shaped to allow them to see things close up and far away at the same time, and because they are positioned on either side of their head, they have almost 340-degree vision.

SWAN

FAMILY: *Anatidae*

DISTRIBUTION: Global distribution covering Europe, Central Asia, North America, Australia and New Zealand

HABITAT: Ponds, rivers, lakes, coastal bays and other wetlands

The annual tradition of Swan Upping happens every year during the month of July on the River Thames. Once a ceremonial event, now it is a five-day census of all the swans in the area, and plays a key role in river conservation, providing an opportunity for each bird to be weighed and checked for injury.

In the tenth century, these birds were seen as luxury goods and any person of worth would serve them as the centrepiece of their feast. King Henry III was a huge fan, and was said to have feasted on forty at one time, during a record-breaking Christmas dinner in 1251 that included 125 roast birds. Luckily, thanks to trading with the American colonies, swan was swiftly replaced on the menu by turkey, but that did not stop it being a status symbol.

In medieval times, wild swans were considered the property of each landowner, and their wings, beak or feet were marked with a unique pattern to denote ownership. Any unmarked bird was the property of the Crown. When Queen Elizabeth I decided she wanted to gather a group together, and was told in no uncertain terms that she had no right, for they belonged to specific landowners, she decided to take the matter to court. It was at this point that a ruling was passed which decreed the queen the rightful owner of any wild swan in the realm, a tradition which is still upheld today.

Being the largest waterfowl species of the Anserinae sub-family, you might think the swan would lumber about, but despite its heavy build and enormous feet, it moves with an elegance that has been likened to a ballet dancer. It inspired Tchaikovsky's famous ballet Swan Lake, whose narrative relies on another feature of the swan's character: its steadfast and enduring love for its mate. When these birds couple up, they usually form lifelong bonds which last many years, and there are numerous tales of one partner dying from a broken heart when they lose the other. In some cases, the pairing will go through a 'divorce', but this is usually when they have failed to successfully breed, and they lose interest in their current mate.

Swans that live in the northern hemisphere have a brilliant white plumage, while those in the south can be black, or black and white. The hue of their feathers goes some way to explain the bird's associations in folklore. Countless mythologies attribute sacred qualities to the white swan, believing it to be synonymous with purity and beauty. The Greek goddess Aphrodite is sometimes depicted in a chariot drawn by swans, while the Celts associate these birds with their goddess of healing and water, Brigid. One of the most famous tales in mythology features Zeus, who falls in love with Leda, the Queen of Sparta, and transforms into a magnificent white swan in a bid to woo her. According to the tale he seduces the queen (although some versions claim he rapes her). The result of their union is an egg which produces two babies, Polydeuces and Helen – who would later become Helen of Troy.

The pre-Christian Celts saw swans as creatures of the Otherworld, able to traverse land, air and water, they were considered magical and held in high regard. One of the most famous Irish tales speaks of the god of water Manannan mac Lir, whose beautiful wife dies shortly after giving birth to four children. When Lir marries again, his new wife instantly dislikes her stepchildren. Encouraging them to swim out to sea, she takes a druid's wand and transforms them into swans, cursing them to this form for 900 years. This concept of shapeshifting is popular, particularly in Celtic mythology, and there are countless folktales of swan maidens who cast off their feathery skin when they reach the shore. Many gullible men have been smitten by their human form, stealing their skin in a bid to hold them captive. This usually ends in disaster, as the maiden retrieves what has been stolen and returns to the sea with any children from the union.

Males are called 'cobs', while the female of the species is a 'pen'.

♦

With a massive 3 m (10 ft) wingspan, swans can fly through the air at speeds of up to 113 km/h (70 mph). They are also nifty swimmers, reaching 2.6 km/h (1.6 mph) by using their powerful webbed feet.

♦

Swans like to stand on one leg for several minutes to absorb heat through their foot, which they tuck beneath their feathers. This helps them adjust their body temperature to suit the environment.

IBIS

FAMILY: *Threskiornithidae*
DISTRIBUTION: Throughout the world, but especially in temperate regions
HABITAT: On the margins of lakes and rivers, swamps, grasslands, wetlands, lagoons and marshes

With fossil records dating back almost 60 million years, the ibis has ancient roots. Primarily a wading bird, it has long spindly legs ideal for standing in the water, and an elongated oval-shaped body and slender neck. The most notable feature of this waterbird is its curved, lengthy beak, ideal for probing the depths and snagging a tasty morsel. Often called the farmer's friend for its ability to consume a range of pests, it is commonly seen on mudflats, lake edges and flooded fields. This bird takes its time, gradually pacing the ground, swaying its beak back and forth to graze the surface. That said, it can be sneaky too, and has been known to steal food from other birds in the flock.

Gregarious in nature, the ibis is all about teamwork and does almost everything in a group, from roosting and foraging to nesting in large colonies which are often mixed with other wading birds. In flight, these birds really impress, working in formation to create precise patterns in the sky that are not only striking but also functional, helping the birds travel with ease. In particular, the V-shaped arrangement reduces wind resistance for those flying at the back, and the birds take it in turns to first lead the flock and then retire to the back to allow time to recharge.

Breeding is also an organized affair, with the males arriving together in a group at the breeding grounds. To attract a mate, the male will likely position himself upon a tree branch and then actively preen and point his beak skywards. He will also make a loud honking noise. Interested females may alight upon the ground, and the male will bow his head at her approach. Sometimes the male will offer the female a twig to prove his ardour. Nests are usually built in the forks of trees, or on clumps of grass and reed beds near other wading birds.

While some might assume that the ibis is awkward in its stance, its slow, steady pace when walking and long, rhythmic wing beats give it grace and poise. No wonder, then, that the ancients were transfixed with this wader. During the Ptolemaic period of Egyptian civilization, the African sacred ibis was a common sight frequenting the swampy areas along the Nile. Avid feeders, these birds eliminated many of the key pests of that time, including snails which infested and contaminated the ponds with parasites, as well as snakes. As such they were revered, and perhaps this was the main reason for their association with the god of wisdom and writing, Thoth. It is thought that the ibis was the form that the deity chose to inhabit the earthly plane and he was often depicted bearing the head of the bird. Some believe this was in part because of the curved beak, which resembled the crescent moon. Indeed, his Egyptian name, Djehuty, translates as 'he who is like the ibis', and just as this wader would dig deep with its sensitive beak to find food, Thoth was synonymous with hidden knowledge.

The birds were regularly mummified in honour of the god, with several million killed and embalmed for this purpose, from around 1100 B.C. The bodies were filled with snails, grain and other sources of food, and then swathed in linen and placed in urns, which were secreted away in underground caverns along the Nile. The custom was to ensure the bird's safe and swift journey onto the afterlife. Ironically, breeding farms soon became the norm to keep a constant supply of these birds available for mummification, but by the mid-nineteenth century, the African sacred ibis became extinct in Egypt.

The bird's fame and providence soon spread throughout ancient Greece and Rome. Here the bird was worshipped and often appeared in artwork adorning buildings and temples. A symbol of wisdom, protection and patience, the ibis still intrigues and delights in equal measure.

The diet of this wader has a direct effect on the colour of its plumage. The bright red feathers of the scarlet ibis come from a diet rich in shrimps.

♦

Most species of ibis have bare parts upon their face, head and chest. These turn bright red during the breeding season.

♦

When they are born, ibises have a straight beak; the curved downward slant only starts to take shape at around two weeks of age.

♦

A group of ibises is called a 'colony' or a 'congregation'. They have also been called a 'unit', thanks to their organized behaviour.

PUFFIN

FAMILY: *Alcidae*
DISTRIBUTION: Found in most of Europe, the Arctic fringes and North
America
HABITAT: Coastal and off-shore waters, rocky islands and at sea

These portly parrots of the sea bring a smile to anyone's face with their colourful antics and comical appearance; no wonder they are called the 'Clowns of the Ocean'. That said, their Latin moniker *Fratercula marina* hails from a more sombre viewpoint. It was thought these playful birds resembled medieval friars, thanks to their fat bellies and dark black back feathers which looked like capes, and so the term, which means 'friars of the sea' evolved. It is also believed that their quirky habit of holding their feet together as they launch beneath the waves looks similar to a monk in prayer. The first written description of these lovable birds appeared in 1570 when their 'puff ball' appearance was noted in much detail, and from this the name 'puffin' was created.

There are four species of these birds in existence: the tufted puffin, the horned puffin, the Atlantic puffin, and the rhinoceros auklet. While they all belong to the same Alcidae family, only four are members of the Fratercula genus. The rhinoceros auklet is the odd one out, and this shows in its appearance. Being grey in hue, it also lacks the broad colourful beak of its counterparts, but it does feature numerous facial adornments, including a small fluorescent horn at the top of its bill. Living along the western coast of North America and also East Asia, it is believed this bird was the original puffin from which all other species are descended.

Puffins pull out all the stops during the mating season, donning their brightest and best colourways in the spring. Their citrus orange feet and beak stand out against the monochrome shading of their feathers. Atlantic puffins go a step further, with a multicoloured bill comprising of a blue base and vivid orange and sunshine yellow stripes. In the winter their beaks are dull and grey, as if to match the change in weather.

While they might look amusing, puffins have a long and mysterious history with humankind and caused great concern during the Middle Ages. Muslim and Jewish scholars were particularly perturbed by the appearance of these birds, believing them to be neither fish nor human, but strangely a little of both. Because of this, they called for them to be killed. The Irish revered the puffin. They refused to eat these birds, believing the sea-bound beauties were sacred, and the souls of deceased Celtic monks. In Iceland, the puffin was also known as the lundi, and a favourite with fishermen, who claimed the bird could predict the weather. It was thought that when a puffin made its way to shore, a storm would swiftly follow. The bird could also predict an abundance of fish, and so its movements were carefully charted each day.

To the Inuit people, the puffin was a friendly spirit who had the power to control the tides and the weather. Beaks were often collected and fashioned into a musical instrument, which when played could heal the sick. The bird was also seen as a spiritual guide who could take on human form and would appear in dreams offering advice and guidance. The Norse favoured this bird, believing it was a reincarnation of their god Thor, gifted with all his strength and ability. The belief that the puffin was the spiritual form of one who had passed was common around the world, and even entered the heart of the Isle of Avalon as the reincarnated guise of King Arthur. The king of legend was said to have appeared as many different creatures as possible, but the puffin was predominant.

Today the puffin's fortunes have faded, for while they are still admired around the world and found throughout the northern hemisphere, numbers have declined dramatically thanks to a lack of prey from over-fishing and climate change. Some populations manage to survive the shifting landscape, but others have dwindled with virtually no pufflings making it to adulthood. The fate of this charming sea bird is undetermined, but its standing in folklore endures.

Pufflings have a huge appetite and can get through approximately 2,000 fish during their thirty-five to sixty-day fledgling period.

♦

Puffins have barbs upon their pallet known as 'denticles'. These tiny spikes keep the fish in place, allowing the bird to hunt for more. Tiny spines along the tongue help to pierce the fish against the denticles.

♦

Puffins struggle to lift into the air and maintain flight. They often crash-land, tumbling headfirst into the water or into other groups of puffins, giving them their clumsy reputation.

♦

Puffins kiss... well, almost! They tap their beaks together during courtship as a way of strengthening pair bonds and showing affection.

COMMON GULL

FAMILY: *Laridae*

DISTRIBUTION: Found on every continent in the world

HABITAT: Farmland, wetland, grassland, marshes, sand dunes, rocky slopes, cliffs and urban areas

Graceful in its movements, the common gull is slighter than its ring-billed cousin and smaller than the insatiable herring gull. In effect, this species is an understated version, being gentler in its approach to life, both on and off the wing. With telltale greenish yellow legs and a bright golden bill, the bird is easy to pinpoint from others of its family. That said, it is still a gull, and has all the common features of such birds, including a raucous laughing call and an opportunist approach to scavenging. The gull's diet is mainly worms, fish and insects, but it also feeds on other detritus, foraging through human waste and gobbling up anything that looks remotely edible.

The moniker 'common gull' gives the wrong impression of this bird, for while gulls do appear to be in abundance, particularly on British shores, in truth this species is not as prevalent as some of the other larger gulls. The name itself was assigned by Thomas Pennant in 1768, and it is thought he was referring to the feeding grounds of this bird, which were usually pastures used for grazing and common land available to all.

There are fifty species of gull around the world and they are all thought to come from one specific water-bound ancestor, a seabird gifted with webbed feet and a body somewhat like a duck crossed with a gull. Fossil evidence from China suggests that this species, named *Gansus yumenensis*, was a waterfowl that existed around 110 million years ago, and that this was the original ancestor of most aquatic birds.

While many complain of the gull's thrifty nature and its ability to swipe a tasty treat from human hands, it is actually proof of the skill, dexterity and intelligence of the bird. All gulls have one thing in common – they have learnt that if they frequent places inhabited by humans, they are more likely to find food which is free, easy and without risk, and so picking up waste and sometimes stealing it from under the nose has become an art form to these tricksters. This gift for the scavenge is something that juvenile gulls learn over time. It is many years before they achieve their adult plumage, with some species taking four years to reach this pinnacle.

Being resilient to environmental changes, and able to withstand a range of temperatures from the freezing cold of the Arctic to the unforgiving heat of the desert, you would think that gulls would be admired for the way they persist against the odds, and yet they have a strained relationship with humankind. Sailing superstitions from around the world cite gulls as the souls of drowned sailors and fishermen. The bird's plaintiff screech is thought to be them crying out to the living, in torment. A similar superstition claims you should never touch or harm a gull, for fear that you will damage the deceased soul in some way.

The ancients had a more favourable view of these birds. The Celtic Sea god, Manannán mac Lir, who featured in Irish mythology, was thought to take the form of a gull. Known as the Lord of the Sea, he would survey his realm in aerial flight, or shift into human form and ride his magical steed, Embarr, across the waves. To the Romans, gulls were a positive omen and a sign that someone would soon return home after travelling across water, while in Chinese mythology the gull teaches an important lesson about love. In a famous folktale, a wealthy man helps a wounded gull, only to become obsessed with it. Instead of letting it fly free, he keeps it in his home and offers it a feast of rich food, but the bird refuses to eat and eventually dies. The moral being that love is about putting the needs of another before your own.

Gulls can drink both fresh and salt water. This ability, which only a few birds have, is thanks to a special gland situated near their eye, which removes salt from their system.

♦

Gulls are excellent mimics. Herring gulls are particularly gifted and able to copy human speech and other artificial noises.

♦

They are not really seagulls. While this is a popular term for birds that live by the coast, gulls live in a variety of habitats, with some never venturing near the sea in their lifetime. Because of this, ornithologists tend not to use 'sea' when referring to a gull.

♦

A group of gulls is called a 'flock' or a 'colony', but other popular terms reference the noise these bird makes, with a 'screech' and a 'squabble' being top of the list.

CURLEW

FAMILY: *Scolopacidae*
DISTRIBUTION: The British Isles, Europe, extending into Scandinavia, Russia and as far east as Siberia
HABITAT: Found on mudflats, estuaries, moorlands, marshes, meadows and arable fields

Strutting along the sand-clogged wetland, its slender blue-grey legs extended, the curlew takes a moment to survey the landscape. Grey and soggy to most, this is the ideal hunting ground for this statuesque wader, particularly the female of the species who prefers sandy mudflats to the grassland foraging of the male. The curlew struggles to thrive at times and breeding figures have dipped over the years, thanks to intensive farming and the loss of moorland habitats. These ground-nesting birds prefer open grassland and bogs to forest environments, where predators can easily hide among the foliage.

The curlew is a migratory bird and can be seen in most countries at different times of the year, but wherever they find themselves, curlews will always migrate to upland areas of heath and rough pasture once the summer has passed.

With buff brown upperparts that are lined with dark streaks, and a creamy off-white mottled belly, their plumage allows them to blend into their surroundings. They are mostly known for the bow-shaped beak which curves in a downwards arch. This fierce-looking appendage is extremely sensitive to touch, and allows them to detect their prey and then prize it gently from the mud, using a pincer-like action not dissimilar to chopsticks.

The first recorded mention of the curlew was in a poem from around A.D. 1000 called 'The Seafarer'. Since then, stories abound of this beautiful bird, with references to its mournful scream which it uses as an alarm call and to display prowess. The 'curl-leap' sound it makes cuts through the air, rising on the second note like a ghostly wail, and it is for this reason that the bird gets both its name and its sometimes strange folklore. In English and Welsh mythology, the call of the curlew was associated with 'The Seven Whistlers'. These were seven birds who would fly together at night and emit an eerie call thought to be an omen of danger and death. It was believed that the haunting sound came from the spirits of the dead, but in truth it was the curlew calling to its mate or warning off other birds. The bush stone curlew, found through Australia, features in many Aboriginal tales, and like its European cousins is synonymous with impending death.

Another tale from folklore paints the curlew in a more positive light. In a seventh-century story, a Welsh missionary named St Beuno was sailing to Anglesey. The waters were choppy and the wind began to batter his tiny boat. St Beuno clung to the sides, and as he did his book of sermons, which he had collected over the years, fell into the ocean. Distraught, St Beuno bowed his head in prayer, and at that moment a brown bird with a long, deeply curved beak swooped in from the shore and dipped below the surface of the waves. As it rose into the air it was carrying the book, which it carefully placed on the rocks to dry. St Beuno was overcome with joy and gratitude, and gave thanks by blessing the bird. He decreed that from that moment on, the curlew would be protected and its nests would always be obscured from human eye.

The genus name for this bird also has special significance. *Numenius* is comprised of two Greek words, 'neos' meaning 'new', and 'mene' for moon. It is thought that the crescent-shaped bill inspired this moniker, coupled with the ethereal call which was often heard beneath the light of the moon.

A group of curlews is called 'a curfew of curlews'; other popular names include 'skein' and 'salon'.

♦

The curlew may have long spindly legs, but these lithe limbs are incredibly strong. Their feet are specially adapted to navigate muddy wetlands and run at speed even when it is sludgy underfoot.

♦

Curlews can predict the weather, according to folklore. If you hear the bird call during the day, rain is on the way. If you are on a boat and you see these birds flying overhead, a storm is brewing.

♦

The Eskimo curlew, also known as the 'prairie pigeon' or 'doe bird', was once a popular inhabitant of North American shores but has not been sighted since the 1980s, leading experts to think it is now extinct.

PENGUIN

FAMILY: *Spheniscidae*

DISTRIBUTION: Every continent, from Antarctica to sub-Antarctic islands, Australia, New Zealand and the coasts of South America

HABITAT: Icy habitats, oceans, coasts and islands

The black and white plumage of the penguin may be instantly recognizable on land, but under water it is uniquely adapted to camouflage them when deep-sea fishing. Along with their monochrome style, penguins have flippers instead of wings, webbed feet and a fusiform body (meaning tapered at both ends), all of which allows for smooth, fluid and effective movement under the water.

A penguin's diet is predominantly fish, squid and krill, which is just as well as the birds can spend months at sea, and favour island, coastal habitats with fewer predators. A solid, thick-built frame with dense bones allows them to sink beneath the waves, unlike other birds who have hollow bones which enable flight.

In total there are eighteen species of penguins, with two of these, the emperor and Adélie, being true inhabitants of Antarctica. The rest tend to favour the northern tip of the Antarctic Peninsula where conditions are a fraction less hostile. Genetic evidence has found that all penguins hail from coastal regions in Australia, New Zealand and the nearby islands of the South Pacific around 22 million years ago. This might sound surprising, but those first penguins made their way to Antarctica and further still, to South America and Africa, around 12 million years ago when Drake's Passage opened up fully. This stretch of water caused the Antarctic current to intensify, and the resulting glaciation forced those species who had not adapted to the icy conditions to move northwards. So the penguins found new homes and evolved.

Warmth is key for a bird that lives in such harsh environments, and it is the reason why they are often seen huddled together in large groups. Their feathers are thick and provide some comfort from the chill, and they have a layer of blubber beneath the skin that holds in warmth while they are under water.

Having such a lovable reputation, it is no surprise that these birds feature favourably in folklore, and are often seen as positive omens and symbols of friendship and joy. The Māoris, in particular, had a penchant for the penguin, and called the Fiordland penguin by the name Tawaki. In mythology, Tawaki was a god who walked the planet in human form. Able to blend in seamlessly, he could be at the heart of humanity unnoticed. It was not until he climbed to the top of a hill, cast off his garments and cloaked himself in lightning, that those around him realized he was a deity. In reality, the Fiordland penguin is only 55 cm (22 in) in height and rather small to be a god, but its flared yellow crest is most likely the reason for this moniker, resembling lightning as it hits the earth.

Penguins are often ridiculed for their waddle, which is also the term used for a group of these birds on land, but ironically the male of the species displays otherworldly strength and courage in the way it looks after its young. In particular, emperor dads withstand some of the worst weather, including freezing temperatures and blizzards, to stand still as statues with the egg and balance their precious cargo on their feet. Should the egg falter and fall upon the ice, the chick would freeze to death. Fasting and no doubt fading from lack of sustenance, these heroic fathers await the return of the female from sea. Even after the chick has hatched and despite the fact he has not eaten for around 125 days, the male remains a permanent presence at his baby's side. When the female finally returns, he is able to go to sea and feed again. Once fattened with fish, the male returns, instinctively drawn to the female's side by the whistle of his chick.

With an average life expectancy of between fifteen and twenty years, and a high mortality rate in young chicks, penguins work hard to maintain their numbers, but climate change is having a detrimental effect. Emperors and Adélie struggle the most, because they need the ice to breed and feed, and as it disappears numbers are dwindling rapidly.

When the Portuguese explorer Ferdinand Magellan (1480–1521) first circumnavigated the globe, one of his crew members spotted a group of penguins in the Falkland Islands and called them 'strange geese', a term which stuck for a while.

♦

The discovery of fossils suggests there was an ancient breed of penguins who were over 1.5 m (5 ft) in height, with some even reaching a colossal 1.8 m (5 ft 10 in).

♦

Penguins have fleshy spines on their tongue and the roof of their mouth. These backward pointing spikes, called 'papillae', are made of keratin and are used to guide fish to the back of the mouth, making it easy to swallow them whole.

GAME
BIRDS

From stark barren landscapes savaged by winter's icy touch to flourishing woodland and wildflower meadows, the birds in this chapter do not fear the shifting environment, for they have learnt to work with it. Adept in the art of subterfuge, these often-portly charmers are masters of disguise, able to merge motionless into the background at the sound of distant footfall. They have adapted over time, like the canny ptarmigan with a quick change of plumage to match snowier surroundings, but while nature is their ally, it is humankind that brings the threat, for these are game birds. Hunted and prized for their feathery worth, some escape the dinner table, but they are revered in other ways, being avians with the most unique skills and talents. Often gifted with beauty and flair, they should never be underestimated, for unlike many other birds they are survivors at heart.

ROOSTER

FAMILY: *Phasianidae*

DISTRIBUTION: Native to the tropical jungles of Southeast Asia, found throughout the world

HABITAT: Mostly domesticated on farms and in coops, in the wild they thrive in shrubland, forests and jungles

The humble chicken, of which the rooster is the male of the species, may not be at the top of everyone's interesting bird list, but its origins stem back 10,000 years with the discovery of fossil bones in northeast China from around 5400 B.C. While these early birds are related to the chickens of today, their wild ancestors hail from India, which suggests they were transported there. The red jungle fowl, known as *Gallus gallus*, is the ancestor of the chicken, and both birds share the red wattle and comb, with males sporting sturdy leg spurs to assert dominance when fighting. Indeed, roosters have a long history when it comes to waging war.

During the fifth century, a battalion of Athenian soldiers were making their way to confront the Persian troops when their general, Themistocles, made them stop to watch two cocks fighting on the roadside. He used this spectacle of strength to inspire his men, claiming that the roosters did not fight for glory or liberty, or for the sake of their children – they fought because one would not give in to the other. The general saw this battle of wills as a lesson in fortitude and his army went on to defeat the invading Persians in the Battle of Salamis (480 B.C.). As such, the chicken, and more importantly the rooster of legend, became an important symbol synonymous with power and virility. Maybe this is why the ancient Greek city of Pergamum created a special arena for cock-fighting. Although illegal in many countries now, it is thought that this is one of the oldest continual sports in the world.

Face-offs aside, no other sound says 'morning' more than the cock-a-doodle-doo of a rooster in full voice. A signature call with a distinct purpose, roosters crow to alert other males that this is their territory. It is a herald for the day ahead which says, 'I'm here, I'm ready, this is mine.' It is also a function governed by their circadian rhythms, the natural instinctive response to time that these supercharged males have within their arsenal, and it explains why they do it at a similar point in the day. Some believe it is the roosters' way of signalling 'forage time' to their flock – after all the males are the leaders of the pack, being puffed up with confidence and virility.

With long, curved tail feathers and a brightly coloured wattle and comb, the rooster is showier than the average hen, making him easy to spot. Young males are called cockerels, but once fully grown take on the regal mantle of rooster or cock.

While roosters may seem bold and somewhat 'cocky' in their approach to life and other males, there is positive side to their presence. Hens within a flock governed by a male often appear calmer. Having a dominant male brings a sense of structure and order to proceedings. Weaker hens tend to flourish, as the rooster's presence means that all the females are equal and this puts an end to in-house squabbling.

Christianity has a less favourable view of the rooster, thanks to the part it played in the disciple Peter's denial of Jesus. According to the passage in the Bible, Jesus states, 'I tell thee, Peter, the cock shall not crow this day, before thou shalt thrice deny that thou knowest me' (Luke 22:34). This appearance made the bird synonymous with betrayal, but while those early Christians may have shuddered at the cock's crow, other mythologies saw it as a signal that the demons of the night had been vanquished.

To the Romans, the rooster was a key motif. Often appearing in artwork and bronze carvings, it was linked to the god of trade and commerce. The Chinese associated the rooster with benevolence, knowledge and courage, and believed that when its call rang through the air, the evil spirits that had plagued the night were gone and all was well with the world.

The ancient Egyptians were the first to artificially incubate chicken eggs. They created chambers connected by vents and corridors and filled them with hundreds of ovens. These were carefully guarded by egg attendants who ensured the heat stayed at a steady temperature using straw and camel dung.

♦

A rooster's testes grow and shrink depending on the season. When there is lots of sunshine, the testes swell and the bird produces more sperm. His wattle and comb also fluctuate seasonally so that he attracts females when he is at his most virile.

♦

If a male is foraging and finds food, he will perform a ritual often called 'tidbitting' which involves him softly clucking while picking and dropping the food on the ground to attract the attention of the hens. He will let them eat first, picking up any leftovers afterwards.

WILD TURKEY

FAMILY: *Phasianidae*

DISTRIBUTION: Native to North America, they have been introduced to various parts of the world including New Zealand

HABITAT: Open woodland, hardwood forests with fields, orchards or marshes

These heavy-bodied ground dwellers are somewhat gangly at first glance, but take a closer look and you will see a noble grace to the way this bird moves. The wild turkey's deportment is partly down to the sturdy legs and the fanned tail feathers which help it balance, but there is a social ease too, which intimates a deeper intelligence. No wonder, then, that Benjamin Franklin, the founding father of the United States, thought it would make a better national emblem than the bald eagle. It was, in his words, 'the epitome of courage and a much more respectable bird'.

First emerging around 300 B.C. and native to the dusty slopes of east and south Mexico, this curious bird caught the eye of those early Mayans who saw an opportunity and a food source which they could harvest. No doubt the iridescent tail feathers of the male were also a draw; coming in a variety of shades from burnished bronze to purple, copper and gold, they were the favoured adornments of headdresses.

Over time the domesticated turkey grew in popularity, with Spanish explorers catching on to its unique taste and taking huge swathes of the birds back to Europe. With a rounded belly to match the curve of its wings, the bird offered ample meat and it was easy to rear too, but it was the turkey's charming personality that elevated its position. Easy to train, the bird adapted to its new surroundings and soon revealed a host of other skills, including acute eyesight and hearing, and a gift for flying. While its appearance seems at odds with a life in the air, in truth the turkey can reach up to 89 km/h (55 mph) in flight for a mile at a time.

Farmers soon took to the character of the bird, with some even keeping their favourites as pets, and the church also gave the heavenly seal of approval, suggesting it should be the dish of celebration and a mainstay at religious festivals. What started as a humble, easy-to-handle bird, available in abundance, became the preferred choice at the table at Thanksgiving and Christmas.

While the turkey had been introduced to Europe by Spanish explorers, the English-speaking world heaped the credit on the Ottoman Empire, believing that most commodities hailed from there. The bird was therefore named 'turkey' after the country, and also because it resembled a type of guinea fowl known as the 'turkey-cock'.

It was an American president who brought the turkey even more acclaim. After taking office in 1861, Abraham Lincoln moved into the White House with his son Thomas, commonly known as 'Tad', who was a rebel at heart, much to the dismay of the long-suffering servants and dignitaries. Tad loved to play pranks, spraying notable guests with the firehose and even selling his father's clothes in a yard sale held on front lawn. But while his constant need for attention caused chaos, he had a deep love for animals, and so when his father brought home the gift of a live turkey for Thanksgiving, Tad made it his pet. The two were inseparable, with the turkey doing what turkeys do best and faithfully following the boy as he strolled through the White House each day. As Thanksgiving passed and Christmas loomed, the president took his son aside to explain that the bird was for eating, but

Tad was having none of it and argued a case for his feathered friend. In the end Lincoln conceded, taking pen and paper and writing a pardon for the turkey – a custom which has become presidential practice ever since, and so the far-from-home bird became a hero of the New World.

The turkey has been deeply embedded in culture and society for a long time, and is synonymous with abundance and the ability to show gratitude for the blessings of life.

Female turkeys are 'hens', while males are called 'gobblers' after the distinctive gobbling call they make to attract a mate.

♦

The fleshy protuberance which hangs above a male's bill is called a 'snood'. Studies have showed that the females prefer a male partner with a larger snood, as this is thought to indicate good health.

♦

Male birds who are related will often court a female together, assisting each other in the chase, but only one will win her favour.

♦

You can tell how a turkey is feeling by the colour of its head. Hues vary from red to blue to white, depending on the strength of their emotion and how excited or chilled they are.

♦

If you want to determine the sex of a turkey, look at its poop. If it is spiral-shaped, then it is likely to be female, whereas poop arranged in a J-configuration is usually male.

PEAFOWL

FAMILY: *Phasianidae*

DISTRIBUTION: Indian peafowl are distributed widely over South Asia, the green peafowl are native to Sri Lanka, and the Congo peafowl can be found in Africa, but they have been introduced all over the world

HABITAT: Open lowland forests, tropical and deciduous forests, farm and agricultural land, parks and cities

Resplendent and regal, the peacock (the male of the species), which is part of the pheasant family, is a beautiful creature blessed with long, slender tail feathers that form a train and can be fanned out into an impressive, shimmering umbrella. Each tip of the upper tail has a stunning eyespot framed with a ring of blue-bronze to accentuate its glory. The females – peahens – are more drab with a blue-green collar but otherwise speckled and brown body.

The blue (or Indian) peacock has body feathers that are bluey-green and metallic in hue. The green peacock has green to bronze body feathers which also glow, and the Congo peacock, which also happens to be the national bird of the Congo, has a bronze-green body with a black underside and tail feather tips which are violet, when fully mature.

Peafowl are native to Sri Lanka and India, and it was the Phoenicians who first carried them to foreign shores, to Egypt and what is now Syria. The ancient Egyptians were immediately taken with this strange-looking creature, especially the eye-shaped pattern on the male birds, which to them was a direct link with the All-Seeing Eye of Horus, a symbol of protection. That said, they were contradictory in their adulation and also associated the bird with the tale of Argus, who locked the goddess Isis away in a tower during the absence of her husband Osiris. Argus had many spies working for him, and had hatched a plan to become king, but when Osiris returned he was swiftly dethroned. As punishment for his sneaky betrayal, he was turned into a peacock and the many eyed tail feathers were a nod to the spies that he had secreted about the kingdom.

The theme of protection is one that is often associated with this bird, and may go some way to explain why European nobles kept them as part of their estate. Adding a unique blend of colour and vivacity to the traditional landscape, they roamed freely throughout their lands. In Islamic folklore the peacock was said to guard the gates of paradise, while the Hindus believed the bird was angel-like in appearance, apart from its ugly feet which were the reason behind its hideous screech. It is thought that each time the bird caught sight of them, it cried out in anguish. Even so, it was sacred to them, and they associated it with beauty, poise and good fortune. Synonymous with the goddess of wealth Lakshmi, peacock feathers were often kept in the home to promote prosperity.

Alexander the Great also had a role to play in the popularity of peacocks, bringing them to Europe. It was thought that when he first caught sight of the bird on the shores of the River Ravi in the Punjab, he was so enamoured by its appearance that he decreed it should be protected and sent back to Greece. The philosopher Aristotle was also taken with the bird, claiming it must be immortal. This theme of the afterlife and resurrection was popular with early Christians, and also with the Romans who often had images of peafowl carved into their catacombs. That said, the sacred link did little to deter them from eating the birds, and they were the lavish centrepiece at many feasts.

The glimmering appearance of the peacock's feathers may go some way to explain its connection with wealth, and why it was so popular with the higher echelons of society. In truth, this iridescence is caused by tiny crystal-like structures that coat some of the feathers and reflect the light when they are spaced out, a feat which can only be seen as the bird grows. Tiny peachicks are drab in comparison to their adult male counterparts, making them hard to tell apart. They do not begin to grow their tail feathers until the age of three. Once fully grown, the male's impressive train can reach up to 1.8 m (6 ft) in length, but despite this weighty appendage peafowl can still fly, even if they are limited on how far and fast they can go.

A family of peafowl is called a 'bevy', and when they gather in large groups they are known as an 'ostentation', a 'muster' or a 'party'.

♦

These clever birds know how to turn heads. When they mate, peacocks unleash a distinctive call, which lets all the peahens in the area know that the male is sexually mature and more experienced than most. This boosts their appeal and draws more partners. Researchers have discovered that a third of mating calls are fake and made to specifically to draw more females.

♦

Peafowl are in it for the long haul. These magnificent birds can live up to twenty-five years in the wild, and up to fifty in captivity.

PHEASANT

FAMILY: *Phasianidae*

DISTRIBUTION: Found worldwide, but native to China and East Asia

HABITAT: Farmland, fields, meadows, marshes, woodland and grassland

There is a crowing sound cutting through the murky grey of dawn. Clear and shrill, it is the call of a male pheasant, a noise issued to assert his dominance or perhaps in alarm. Portly and pear-shaped in body, the pheasant has a long, thin tail which is strikingly barred in the male. He also has iridescent plumage with chestnut-golden back feathers, the deepest fern-green head and red wattling upon his cheeks, which makes him an easy target in the undergrowth. No wonder this bird rarely lives beyond a year in the wild. The female stands more of a chance; being buff brown in colour with dark markings, she can blend seamlessly with her surroundings.

Native to Asia, it is thought that the common pheasant originated in the forests of southeast China. The species evolved with time, and around 4.3 million years ago it diverged, separating the green pheasant from the common variety. The Romans helped the spread of the bird by bringing it to European shores. Phoenician traders also played their part, and soon the pheasant became a popular game bird among the higher classes. For a while after, its prevalence wavered and it seemed to disappear from UK shores, but in 1059 King Harold made the pheasant popular again. As a mark of the privilege of office, it was customary to offer the canons of Waltham Abbey a brace of partridge, but he switched things up and offered pheasant instead. This one simple act changed the fate of the bird and once again it was sought after.

The Normans served pheasant at their banquets and passed a law to protect the birds, but this swiftly changed and by the time of King Henry I, they were once again in the firing line. With shooting for sport becoming more common in the 1500s, pheasant numbers dwindled and by the seventeenth century they were so depleted that they almost ceased to exist. To combat this, the Chinese ring-necked pheasant was introduced to Europe and by the nineteenth century hunting was in full swing again. Dogs and people took great delight in scouring the hedgerows, scaring the birds from hiding so they could be shot.

More than just another game bird, in truth the pheasant has mastered the art of subterfuge. While it spends most of its life on the ground, this does not make it an easy catch. Gifted with excellent sight and hearing, it can usually detect predators in advance, and will run up to 16 km/h (10 mph) or if startled burst skywards in a 'flush', which can reach up to 97 km/h (60 mph). Usual flying speeds settle at around 56 km/h (35 mph), but this bird does not always rely on the sky for escape; being able to go several days without food, it can stay in hiding until its pursuer loses interest.

While life on Earth can be dicey for the average pheasant, it fares much better in the astral realm, as Japanese ancients will attest. According to early scriptures, a fiery red aura set the skies alight over Japan, in the year A.D. 620. This strange formation resembled a pheasant, a fact which did not go amiss with scholars and mystics. From this moment on the game bird was revered, thought to be a heavenly messenger and cohort of the gods. In particular, the bountiful sun goddess Amaterasu favoured this bird and was thought to have created it to be her emissary. The sacred connotations of the pheasant may go some way to explain why it was named the national bird of Japan in 1947. Called the 'kiji' in Japanese, it is thought that the green pheasant has the ability to sense earthquakes before they happen, and has in the past saved many lives by alerting villages and towns with its odd behaviour.

In China, the golden pheasant with its rainbow colouring was thought to be descended from the mythical phoenix, and because of this it was considered auspicious. Hugely popular at the time of the Qing Dynasty, high-ranking nobles were often seen wearing robes that featured this flamboyant-looking bird. It also had an influence on the mystical creature known as the fenghuang. This mythical bird-like being had the head of a pheasant, the back of a tortoise, the neck of a snake and the tail of a fish. This strange combination was a fortuitous omen, and would appear in dreams or visions and foretell the coming of a new emperor.

Male pheasants, known as 'roosters', have a harem of several hens which they keep safe during the mating season. This gives them the best chance of procreating and then protecting their brood – it also keeps them very busy.

♦

Pheasants pant like dogs. They do not have sweat glands so when they get hot, they breathe rapidly to expel excess heat.

♦

Pheasants will eat almost anything, including fruit, seeds, grain, berries, leaves, ant eggs, worms, caterpillars, grasshoppers, small lizards, voles and even some small birds.

Further Reading

If you want to delve further into the world of birds, the following books and websites offer a host of information, delightful facts and stories to enjoy.

Books

The Life of Birds, David Attenborough, BBC Books, London, 1998
The Wisdom of Birds: Essential Life Lessons for Positivity and Grace, Alison Davies, LOM Art, London, 2024
RSPB Pocket Birds of Britain and Europe, DK books, London, 2022
The Secret Language of Birds: A Treasury of Myths, Folklore and Inspirational True Stories Adele Nozedar, HarperElement, London, 2006
The Urban Birder, David Lindo, Bloomsbury, London, 2011

Websites

audubon.org
bto.org
fatbirder.com
rspb.org.uk
theurbanbirder.com

Acknowledgements

I would like to thank all the wonderful team at Leaping Hare, from the amazing Monica Perdoni who is such a joy to work with and a great champion of my ideas, to my editors Sophie Lazar and Charlotte Frost for their help in shaping and creating this beautiful book. I would also like to thank Sarah Wildling for her fantastic illustrations, which capture the unique spirit and essence of each bird. A huge amount of gratitude goes to Mother Nature for inventing the winged wonders within these pages, and for inspiring me and countless others every day!

Biographies

Alison Davies is a story-teller and writer who runs workshops at universities throughout the UK on how stories and narratives can be used as holistic tools for teaching, healing and learning. She has a keen interest in folklore, wellbeing, and nature and is the author of *Tales Behind the Tarot, Goddess Stories* and *Floral Folklore* (Leaping Hare Press).

Sarah Wildling is an illustrator and pattern designer living in North Yorkshire. She creates hand drawn artwork inspired by flora, fauna and a little bit of magic. She is the illustrator of *Floral Folklore* (Leaping Hare Press).
https://sarahwildling.com @sarah_wilding

Index

Quarto

First published in 2025 by Leaping Hare Press
an imprint of The Quarto Group.
One Triptych Place, London, SE1 9SH
United Kingdom
T (0)20 7700 9000
www.Quarto.com

A catalogue record for this book is available from the British Library.

ISBN 978-0-7112-9846-0
EBOOK ISBN 978-0-7112-9847-7

10 9 8 7 6 5 4 3 2 1

Book Designer: Dinah Drazin
Commissioning Editor: Sophie Lazar
Editorial Director: Jenny Barr
Illustrator: Sarah Mitchell
Senior Designer: Renata Latipova
Senior Editor: Charlotte Frost
Senior Production Controller: Rohana Yusof

Printed in China